D1081810

Jesus Unplugged:

Finding God's Light
Outside Religion

By Rachel Victoria

Copyright © 2019 All rights reserved.

No part of this publication can be reproduced or transmitted in any form or by any means, electronic or mechanical, without permission in writing from the author or publisher.

This book is a memoir. It reflects the author's present memory and understanding of her experiences. Some details, names and characteristics have been changed, events have been compressed, and dialogue has been created.

ISBN-13: 978-1-951407-10-0 Paperback
ISBN-13: 978-1-951407-11-7 eBook

Dedication

For the sensitive souls of today,
who are ready to walk through liberation's door.

Table of Contents

Introduction

I live shrouded but I exist in plain sight.

Those were words that came to me during a morning walk. It felt like the perfect way to describe how I was living, feeling and moving in the world. While people can see me going about my day to day, my truth and my inner life have always been hidden. The time has now come to reveal them.

Ever since I can remember, I had a feeling there was more to Life than what the eye could see. The idea took shape when I was a child. Things at home were sometimes unstable, but when I went outside walking in the fields behind my house and played with my pets, I felt a rare inner peace. Though I couldn't put a name to it, it felt like there was a mystery out there, something greater than myself, that needed to be solved.

Throughout childhood and early adulthood, those kinds of feelings and experiences became common. I had vivid experiences that others didn't. Sometimes it was visions of people who weren't there—especially ghosts. Other times, it was a sense of things that would happen before they actually did. But those feelings never went away. I always felt sensitive. In fact, as I continued to be curious about the meaning of life and the existential question of why we were all here, I experienced a spiritual awakening that became more and more prevalent and demanded my attention.

I started to recognize I was highly intuitive; that I had spiritual gifts that others around me didn't. Even when I was young, I could look out at creation and feel connected to a source, a field that so many others seemed to ignore. Though it took time, I realized that this source was always there within us as a guidepost and refuge.

Although challenging experiences can make life seem shrouded, a more enriched and deeper understanding of Life is always right at our fingertips. Put another way, God (for me with a big G) is always there within us—though maybe by putting a name to it, I've already lost some of you.

I would encourage you not to focus on names, but to stay attuned to my story and the message. Mapping spiritual terrain can be challenging, and putting firm names on things can make it even more so. After all, we are all at different points along the path back to where we came from, guiding each other home.

What is definitely true is that we're in the middle of a spiritual crisis at the moment. People, especially those in the younger generation, are looking for deeper meaning. People are feeling betrayed or let down by the religions in which they were raised. Some are discarding the idea of spirituality altogether.

If that seems bleak, maybe it's better to reframe it as the necessary growing pains that come with an expanding spiritual consciousness. It's a truth I can speak to only because I've lived it.

Through all the hills and valleys in my life, I've become aware of a source or positive presence, particularly after going through marital separation and divorce. But to understand how that could even happen, we need to start at the beginning.

We need to start with who I was when I was just a curious little girl. A girl who didn't go to church, who knew there was something out there but who kept away from it. As I explored the world and myself, it felt like I was straying from a source of goodness that I somehow knew existed, and I had a kind of spiritual breakdown. Another way to say it is that I had a spiritual breaking *in*.

After that moment, everything started to change.

The Truth about the world and parts of my life that were shrouded were revealing themselves to me in waves. I felt lighter and freer—but I was also flattened with devastation and shock. I had details, images and sensations of painful childhood trauma revealed to me in crystal clarity—through dreams, meditations, yoga and downloads from my Higher Power.

After wrestling with it physically, spiritually, mentally and emotionally, I also found healing, which for me meant integration. With practice, I realized I could and needed to raise my vibration more and more. As it turned out, I'd never strayed off any kind of path at all; the path I'd taken was the right one for me.

Over time, I realized I was being summoned to be a messenger for a loving energy and Spirit in the form of written words; that when I was born, I was made as a kind of spiritual channel. As I've come to know Him, the being I call Jesus (after all, He appears to me in that form) has left me feeling seen, loved and understood. We've had deep exchanges and conversations about so many matters of the heart and Spirit.

This is my story, the story of a girl who went out looking for God everywhere, and eventually found Him inside herself.

This book will talk about the personal and surprising relationship I've had with Jesus, unplugged from religion, and the direct messages—or the Divine Downloads—that I've received as a result. But this isn't a book like most religious or Jesus-centric books.

You don't have to be a Christian to read it—in fact, many of the experiences I went through might shock a stereotypically religious person. I encourage you to be as skeptical as you want, but to keep an open mind. This isn't a dogmatic book because the spiritual world isn't dogmatic—it's alive, in flux and in communion with us all the time.

The path I took is not the path all people need to take. In fact, I probably wouldn't recommend it. Still, the conclusions and insights it led to are undeniably true for me. For anyone who has struggled with extreme trauma or its resulting behaviors of self-harm and addiction, my hope is that some of these hard-won insights may provide a map to spiritual recovery and some deeper healing.

My earliest experiences led me to the extreme end of the spectrum when it comes to spiritual exploration. Though the things I've gone through made me the person I am today, I don't think going as far as I did is necessary to have a better relationship with God.

But we can all definitely use a better relationship with a God of our understanding.

I realize that to claim I "channel Jesus" means some people are going to throw eggs at me. I'm mentally and physically prepared for that. My life might change from this book, or it might not. But my intention is to serve, to live on purpose and to help and change people's lives for the better.

As I've said, there's a huge spiritual disconnect on a lot of levels that comes from an old paradigm. My hope is this book will create a beautiful ripple in consciousness and time. Spirituality is definitely vital to recovery of any kind, but we have so many misconceptions about it.

They are similar to the misconceptions and misunderstandings about the second coming.

I had a very vivid dream one night about it, though not in the sense you usually hear about—there was no apocalypse and Jesus didn't take just the "good" people to heaven. The truth is Jesus's first coming to Earth was the awakening of Christ consciousness; the capacity for acceptance and unending Love. That Love lives on today as a potential seed we all carry in our hearts. As one of my old friends used to say: "We are all gardeners of Spirit."

In the new paradigm, the second coming is the reawakening of that consciousness within us, the awakening to our own Christ Light in our hearts.

It's a deep Love and Compassion, which comes in turn from deep self-love and self-compassion first. It's an abiding, sustaining force that makes distractions and harmful behaviors like addiction and abuse unnecessary.

It's the Light, the Love and the guiding energy of Jesus, unplugged from religion.

At the end of the day, all I hope to do is share my story and my insights—about who I was, who I became and who I am now. There are hills and valleys along the way, as well as frightening revelations. There are also choices and insights that might scare some people, but there's nothing to fear.

You can take what resonates and leave what doesn't. As I've discovered over the course of a lifetime, there is no one path set out for all of us to follow.

True spirituality is about honoring all paths. And this one is mine.

Part One

Chapter 1

The Tip Toes House

I was raised as an immigrant, but not in the way you might think.

I was actually born in England, as the middle child to English parents. They emigrated my two siblings and me to a small rural village in one of the coldest parts of Canada right before my fourth birthday. My older brother, Mark, was seven, and I remember him getting sick to his stomach on the long flight. It was the first time I'd ever been on an airplane.

When we landed, we had to wait a long time before we were even allowed off the plane. A Canadian doctor and some other people in uniform inspected me. Even though I was with my family, I was cold, frightened and tired. I huddled with my sister Kate who was just 20 months younger. We always stuck together.

It was the 1970s, so there was no Internet to prepare us for the move to a foreign country. The first place we settled down was like a little Italy, a small Italian neighborhood just north of Toronto. My only friend was a little girl who lived a few doors down from me. Her parents were curious about us, talking in animated Italian while we played—though they spoke no English, my little friend did.

That home in Little Italy was just temporary while our family was getting settled, and a year later, we moved to the Canadian countryside. The house we lived in there was a Victorian country manor; a relatively well-known historical home in Ontario called the Tip Toes House. It was a beautiful and magical place.

We were five miles north of the school district in a town so tiny it was technically called a mews—a house at the end of a country road on two acres surrounded by trees, fields and farmers. The home itself was spacious with a strange floor plan and plenty of places to hide. Some rooms were clad in old repurposed barn board and there was a pool. Because my mum was such an avid English gardener, the walkways and garden beds were parterres, always full of bright flowers and entrancing aromas. My parents rarely had visitors and work colleagues over, but when they did, everyone would comment on how lovely the house and garden were—they were even featured in a hardcover book about homes and gardens.

The summers were particularly idyllic. The grounds had a small cottage and a barn, which we rented out to local blacksmith named Lee. I spent a lot of time around Lee and his girlfriends as a child—mainly because I loved to roam with his adorable goat named Becky. I felt like he was an older brother to me, more so than even my own brother. As many country families do, we gradually collected a lot of animals. Over the years, there was a family mule named Jenny, Lee's horses, about nine cats and our dog Clyde.

I remember my grandfather, with whom I share the same birthday, sending me $20 in the mail, which I used to buy my first rabbit. My brother named her Tootsu, though how to actually spell that is anyone's guess—I don't think we ever wrote her name down! My grandfather was the sweetest gentleman, always properly dressed and buttoned-up with a thick Scottish accent. I treasured the few times he and my grandmother would come visit. After all, we didn't know anybody well and had no other family in Canada.

On one visit, I caught my grandfather walking away from our house down a long road leading to a mews called Elizabeth Square. He was all dressed up with a walking cane in hand. I ran to catch up with him and asked where he was going.

"Oh, Rachel!" he said in his brogue, "I'm off to Sunday church." I didn't know what that meant exactly, but I knew I wanted to go with him. I must have only been nine or 10, but we set off together walking a mile down the road, to the old stone church.

At that time, my mother's critical view of religion had already been instilled in our family of five.

"Religion is bad," she would say. "It only divides people."

Still, I was so curious.

I sat in the pew next to my grandfather, looking up into the intricate stone eaves, the singing reverberating around me. It was my first time ever in church, and while I didn't fully understand all the churchy stuff, I felt a kinship with him in that moment. It wasn't as sinister as my mum had made it out to be.

***

There are huge holes in my memories of childhood. I often can't remember the specifics, but I generally re-member the feelings. There are a select few memories that are very concrete, like the colors of the carpet in our house in England and the time I spent at my Auntie's house when I was three years old.

We had a basically "normal" middle-class British up-bringing—it just happened to take place mostly in Canada. There was a formality and a tradition to life. For lack of a better word, there was a bit of snobbery about proper behavior and appearances.

We were to do what we were told. There would be no questions asked, no back-talking. It was a "no lip" rule, as my parents would say. There wasn't much space allowed for expressing emotions. If one of us fell and skinned our knees, what followed would be a very stiff upper lip.

"Come on now, don't cry," my mother would say. "Get up, carry on." While I was bleeding, someone would make a joke: "Rachel made a hole in the road with her knee!"

Self-deprecating humor and sardonic wit were cover-ups for a lot of things. And much was considered off-limits. "There are certain things that just aren't appropriate," my parents would explain to us. "They aren't proper." The social rules were subtle, complicated and unclear. But if we broke any of them, we'd be in big trouble.

Though my parents and their ways were a little hard to embrace, most of my childhood memories are still imbued with love for them. My father had graduated from Oxford and followed that up with a Master's degree from Stanford. He worked long hours as an executive at a large Canadian company.

My mother had gone to cosmetic school in England, but in Canada, she stayed at home to take care of the house, the garden and her three young children. Meanwhile, my father's career grew and grew. My parents provided us with more than the essentials—we were exposed to the arts, we always had nice clothes and we went on fancy vacations.

As I said, it was a very middle-class British existence.

It was always just the five of us, and my parents didn't socialize very much. They had a few friends here and there and sometimes hosted corporate holiday parties, but everyone was kept at arm's length. An emotional distance marked all of our relationships, as well as my parents' adult lives. My mother, in particular, didn't seem to know how to nurture any friendships. She would love her friends one day and hate them the next.

Though my mum was moody at home, she would turn into a completely different person in any social setting, when she had a dry martini with two olives in her hand. She became the perfect hostess and socialite, the life of the party. She seemed to be a kind, good-looking lady with well-behaved and well-dressed children. She had everything that mattered most to her in the world.

I remember being confused by the uneven affection my parents showed us children. My mum often seemed indifferent towards us. On the other hand, my father was affectionate in his own way—he just saved most of it for my little sister, the baby of the family. I often remember wanting him to *just pick me*, but my mum would get jealous whenever my father showed us too much attention, which just made the dynamic even more complicated.

The simplest way to explain my family is that everything always felt a little off.

My mum was emotionally unavailable to a certain extent. She and my father would argue—about who knows what—and she would spiral into all kinds of angry and irrational behaviors. I remember her slamming doors, storming out of rooms, stonewalling in the middle of arguments. Though our home was generally peaceful and we were provided for, there was always a spiky undercurrent. Sometimes, things would turn unexpectedly ugly.

Whenever my mum would get mad at us children, she would pull out her wooden spoon and smack the backs of our hands. She called us "ragamuffins" and "little besoms," a word that literally means "broom" but that carries nastier connotations for little girls in the British dialect. By the same token, she would dote on us on special occasions like Christmas, Easter and birthdays. As with her friends, she would love us one day and hate us the next.

My mother was very emotionally volatile and my father tried to be the peacemaker. But he had his angry spells, too. He was often called in to do the serious disciplining, typically spankings with a wooden hanger or sometimes a leather belt. Though he could be a fearsome man, he grew kinder and gentler as he aged.

***

Because our family was so geographically isolated, I was excited to make new friends right away when school started.

My first real exposure to Canadian culture was through the school system. I went to a Montessori school for kindergarten. Maria Montessori, a child psychologist and researcher who wanted a more scientific and creative learning method for kids, developed the whole system. A side effect of the Montessori school system was that things were hands-off. Teachers wouldn't do anything for kids that they could do for themselves. Nobody would bend to tie your shoes or help you out—you had to do it on your own.

For Grades One through Eight, I went to the local public school. And perhaps as a result of being from another country, there was bullying and teasing that sometimes went unchecked. The adjustment was rough. The children started making fun of my accent on the first day of Grade One, all of them laughing amongst themselves, imitating my voice and pointing at me behind my back. The experience was short-lived, because as I remember it, I came home and lost my accent within 24 hours. The worst was in Grade Two when some mean girls tied my hair to the monkey bars. I cried and cried until the teacher finally came and untied me. Experiences like that made me feel sad, unloved and small. I hated being picked on and not being able to stand up for myself. I hated not having a loud enough voice. I hated not being able to scream.

But things were worse at home than they were at school.

If my mum was the main antagonist of my childhood, my brother was definitely the second. I was petrified of him. He pushed me around and bullied me almost daily. I was three years his junior, tiny and fairy-like, and he was much taller than me. When he finished growing, he was 6'1" and played high school football. There could be no fair physical contest between us; he would always win. Because my younger sister was even smaller than I was, I also ended up being her protective human shield.

When I was five or six, it started as roughhousing gone wrong—my brother would kick me, sit on me and hold me down. It was harder than would be normal or appropriate, and I complained to my mum and dad. Still, they did nothing to intervene.

"It's because he's an older boy with a lot of energy and idle hands," my mum would say. "He's isolated and he needs someone to play with." We were mostly stuck inside six months of the year because of the cold winters, after all.

No matter how much I protested, it didn't seem to matter. Mark always wanted to wrestle and fight, and Kate and I had to run away. We had board games and TV in the house, but it was never enough to keep him entertained. As a result, a lot of my childhood was spent hiding from my brother just to stay physically safe.

We used to play a game Mark made up called "Fang and Vicious Against the World." I was Fang, my sister was Vicious and my brother was the world. He was tall and strong and I was waifish; my sister was more heavy-set. We had no choice but to play by fighting against him, and it always felt like we were struggling for our lives. Because my brother was the most rebellious and violent of the kids, he would also get the most physical punishment from my parents, who couldn't control him. It was a brutal cycle.

In the summers when we got a little older, we would all ride our bikes a mile down the road to a baseball diamond to meet our friends. There was a tree there that dropped crab apples, and we would pick them up and throw them at one another. Though it was usually all in good fun, there was a seriousness to the play between my brother and I that had a life or death intensity. Mark would pick up crab apples and whip them at my body and my face. I would have huge purple and black bruises, and most of the time, I'd have to get on my bike and ride home to safety.

One time at Christmas, he threw a pinecone at my eye and scratched my cornea. It was so painful that I had to wear a patch over it, along with protective sunglasses while my eye healed. A week later, I was finally able to take the patch off. No sooner had the eye healed than my brother did the exact same thing all over again, and I was back in a patch. I still remember that physical pain like it was yesterday.

No matter what he did, there were no serious reprimands or punishments—at least nothing that changed the behavior.

One time we were swimming in our pool and Mark came up behind me and held me underwater. Maybe it started as play, but it quickly turned into him trying to drown me—or to prove that he *could* drown me whenever he wanted. I remember flailing underwater, panicking and losing all my air while my brother's hands easily kept my little body at bay. He would hold my head down and then take his foot and kick me down even deeper. Black fear coursed through my veins. *This is it,* I thought. *This is how I'm going to die.* Right before everything turned black as I went under, he would let me go and I'd paddle for my life back to the surface for air. I was helpless.

Despite all the mean things Mark did to me, I desperately wanted him to see me as a human being with feelings and sensitivities—not just a human punching bag. But things only progressed.

One time, he shoved me into a window and the side of my head broke the glass, right in front of my father. Even so, the behavior was dismissed.

The worst of all was one summer day. I was sitting in a bikini inside, near the door leading to our pool. Outside surrounding the pool area, there was your usual concrete. The concrete was covered with a thin, red torn and faded fabric, like felt. Because of the Canadian climate and the harsh bristles, the rug was pretty rough. Mark wanted me to go swimming with him and I refused. So, he pulled me off my chair and dragged my body outside, kicking and screaming, over the rough rug and into the pool. I had rug burns all over my body.

The chlorinated pool water stung my raw skin. There were no adults around. None of it seemed to matter.

There was so much emotional chaos in my house, the only times I had a sense of calm were when I was outside in nature with my animals. Even in 20-degree winter weather, I'd put on my cross-country skis and explore the property by myself. I didn't care how cold it was. Something about the clear, clean air put me at peace. It was so picturesque. I felt like I was skiing inside a snow globe.

Outside of those moments, I was afraid of everything. I was afraid of feeling fragile, of being breakable. I was afraid of feeling like I didn't belong in my own family and of being unloved. Most of all, I was afraid of not being protected by my parents. And I was afraid to fully feel how unsafe I actually was.

I kept as active as I could to keep my mind off things and made friends with the neighboring kids and my classmates. Still, the fear inside me bubbled over constantly. My posture became smaller and my voice more remote.

I needed to find my voice again and to speak up for myself if I was going to survive. I felt like if I didn't find my voice, I might lose it forever.

One summer when my brother was about 13, he had a bunch of his friends over. We were all lounging in the front of the house on the stone driveway, and they were on their bikes. They were laughing and joking around with my brother.

"Hey Rachel," one of them yelled, hitting Mark on the arm, "why don't you take your top off for us?" They were all giggling, and everyone turned to see what I would do next.

Something inside me broke open. I was flooded with electricity.

My brother wasn't saying anything in response. I looked him right in the eyes. I held the gaze for as long as I could, trying to send him all the feelings of how much he'd betrayed me. "I'm not doing that," I said, and I walked away.

I think it was the first time I had ever said "no" to anybody.

Everything in our childhood home was twisted together, so enmeshed with unspoken anger and abuse. My only safe places were outside at the barn with Lee and the animals, or out in the snow on my skis. When my mum called us in for dinner, her voice would be so far away I could pretend I was someone else for just a few moments.

For the longest time, I saw no way out. Still, my life was the only Life I knew and nothing about it seemed that unusual. It was just the way things were.

When you are young, the things that happen feel like they are supposed to, and that they always will. I thought my inability to protect myself and my boundaries were facts: I was who I was, and I couldn't change. But that summer day with my brother opened up some space in me. In the strength of that moment, it was like everything I'd been through had been waiting, gathering power to push me out of one way of being into another.

There was a window opening; time was passing and things were changing after all, even if I hadn't noticed. I knew that if I just kept going somehow, good things might be waiting for me on the other side.

Chapter 2

Finding a Voice

My brother graduated from school and my parents sent him to St. Thomas College, a boys' boarding school spanning Grades Nine through 13. After 10 long years, things in our house were finally relatively calm. I got a taste of the safety I'd craved for so long.

Though I'd always been an okay student, having Mark out of the house freed up a lot of mental space. My grades and my confidence improved, and I slowly started coming out of my shell. I started playing basketball and got pretty good—in Grade Eight, I even made the local Regional Championship Team. I started playing the clarinet, too, and loved it right away.

Something about music soothed me the same way nature did.

My family had always been pretty musical. Growing up, my parents told us all kinds of stories about our musical history. My uncle, who lived in England, had taught Brian May, the lead guitarist of Queen, how to play. Later on, when somebody interviewed May and asked him to name the best vocalist he knew—he answered with my uncle's name.

Given the fact May already knew Freddie Mercury at that point, it seemed pretty impressive.

Some of my dad's brothers in England were even in an '80s new wave band called Sail Falling. They had a song that hit number one on the charts in 1980!

Then there were the stories my mum told. She said there was always a racket across the street coming from the pub while she waited for the bus as a young lady. As it turns out, it was The Rolling Stones playing before they were famous.

In any event, music seemed to be a talent I inherited.

After a while, my music teacher, Ms. Frooman, started to take an interest in me. I was highly sensitive and aware and therefore an emotionally mature girl, and my teacher seemed to notice. Though I spent so much of early school trying not to be noticed, I could see her seeing me. She told me I was talented and sensitive, that I had a great ear and played well. Her praise started in Grade Six, but continued through Seven and Eight as well.

When the time came to graduate, she even recommended to the other teachers and faculty that I be the class valedictorian.

I was shocked. I was the last person anyone would expect to be valedictorian—after all, the valedictorian was usually the student with the highest grades or a star athlete. I was a B+ student, and not the smartest or the most athletic. Even so, Ms. Frooman was persuasive, and she must've worked on the rest of the faculty on my behalf. At the end of her campaign, I got to stand up in front of the whole school and give a valedictory speech.

She had a big effect on how I saw myself. I'm not sure if I gave much thought about how other people saw me, but I knew my teacher had seen me as a real person. It gave me confidence. Though I had grown quickly as a girl and was tall for my age, I was still stooping around to seem smaller. That day in front of all my classmates, I was sure to stand myself up tall and to project my voice.

My chin was up. I was starting to feel a little better about myself.

***

After I graduated, it was time for me to go to boarding school like my brother.

In England, it's customary for upper and middle class families to send their kids away to boarding school, for both middle and high school. Because of the cost and timing, my parents had decided we would only go beginning in Grade Nine.

The school I went to was Haversham in Toronto, which was actually a sister school of St. Thomas College for boys. Having a boarding school in the middle of a big city was unusual. Though it was a Canadian school, it had plenty of international students. One of my best girlfriends at the time was from Argentina, another was from China and another was from Mexico. Right away, I knew this would be completely different from the world I'd grown up in. There were people from everywhere, and nobody knew me.

It was a chance to start all over.

Haversham lodged students in a bunch of different boarding houses. There was one house for seventh and eighth graders. After that, the ninth graders all lived in Victorian homes in downtown Toronto. There were separate housing arrangements for the 10th graders and a combined house for the 11th and 12th graders. Finally, there was a 13th Grade as well, which also got its own house.

At the time, Canada was in the middle of getting rid of Grade 13, so my high school career was a little strange. Instead of doing all five full years, I decided to do the "fast track" program, which combined years 11 and 12. Though the arrangements changed later on, I lived in the school's housing for Grades Nine and 10, visiting home on the weekends.

The main thing I remember is the freedom. Because my other school had Grades One through Eight all in one place, all the students had known each other from early childhood. While that was nice for developing close friends, it was also a little boring after a while. It was nice to have a chance to meet new people—and it was so good to be away from my mother.

From the very beginning, I was coming out of my shell. I let my inner rebel come out, and I tested people's boundaries—with my teachers and my housemother. I started asking myself questions about who I was and how

I could be. *Can I be outgoing and friendly?* I wondered. *Can I be funny?*

I tried out for basketball in Grade Nine but got cut, which seemed unfair since I'd been so good in middle school. Still, I kept playing clarinet in the school band. Because we were such a small private school, there was no division between orchestra and band—it was all just one thing. What was even better was that I ran for president of my boarding house that first year and won! I felt so empowered.

Like most girls that age, I started to get attention from boys. Around the same time, I began doing a little bit of modeling as a hobby and a way to make some money. I modeled at local events, like mall fashion shows, and had fun drawing some recognition that way.

When I was about 15, I met my first boyfriend, Pete. He was two years older than me, and I met him through my brother. He was the sweetest boy and he treated me well. I remember getting an emerald green taffeta dress made to go with him to semi-formal at his school—it was a big deal. He even wore a kilt!

We dated for a while, and I even brought him home to meet my parents. Though my dad seemed to like him, my mother found ways to undermine me. I remember one time she drove Pete home without me, as he had broken his ankle and couldn't drive. He later told me she made comments to him about our relationship during the car ride.

"You know, you're going to lose Rachel one day," she said to him. "Either to me or to someone else." He was shocked.

When I confronted my mum about it, she shrugged it off and said it hadn't happened. I even called Mark into the room and told him about it. Although I'd always known our mother to be secretly vindictive, my brother never believed me.

"Why would she say that though, Rachel?" he asked me.

"I don't know!" I said, exasperated. "I told you, she's evil!"

Pete's older brother was best friends with Mark. Because my brother knew Pete through his brother, he knew that Pete wouldn't be dishonest about something like that. It was maybe the first time that my brother started to take my side and believe me about the things I'd said about our mum.

My mother had a tendency in general to overstep boundaries. When Pete and I were together around her, she would sometimes make inappropriate comments about my body or the way I dressed. She ran two small women's clothing stores in Canada, stores she'd opened when I was 11. It started as general retail, but she changed it over to women's lingerie when I was 13, expanding into a second location when I was 15. She would buy me lacy French lingerie and other revealing outfits.

"This is perfect for you, Rachel," she'd say. I would burn with embarrassment.

Other times, she had me come to her stores and try on all kinds of lingerie and bathing suits for the other people who worked there. It felt like she was putting my body on display for everyone. I could often sense an underlying jealousy she had for me. She was the evil queen and I felt like a stepdaughter.

My relationship with Pete lasted a year, but we ended on good terms and stayed friends. At 16, I started dating a boy named Jerry who was six years older than me. I met him modeling at a Benetton fashion show in Toronto. Backstage, all the models were changing together, and Jerry was among them. Boys and girls were usually kept on separate sides, but there wasn't enough space. As a result, Jerry and I had to change right next to each other. It was unusual, but it led to us exchanging numbers, doing a photo shoot together and starting a relationship.

My mum didn't like him at all. She didn't like that he was older, I think, but I don't think it really mattered. No matter what, any young man taking interest in me was not going to win her approval.

***

Around Grade 10, my parents started remodeling the Tip Toes House and bought a townhouse near our high school. Because they were only going to live there for less than 12 months and it was so close to the school, they suggested that my sister Kate and I live in the new house instead of boarding again. We were more than excited.

After that initial year, my mum would stop by from time to time, but we mostly had the entire place to ourselves. We became "day girls" instead of boarding girls, and in the social hierarchy at our school, being a day girl was definitely better.

I kept dating Jerry throughout the rest of school and focused on life outside the home. The summer when I was 16, I started hanging out with a modeling girlfriend and drinking too much. Then I got mono. How it happened was a bit of a mystery to me. Though Mark had it a year before, I didn't know anyone else who had mono. It started on Labor Day weekend and got progressively worse. The glands in my neck were so swollen that I had no chin. I had no energy whatsoever. I remember being so fatigued just walking downstairs in my parents' townhouse that I sat down at the bottom and fell completely asleep.

In all, I was sick for about six weeks and missed a lot of school. When I finally came back, I was out of the loop. My friends were talking about traveling for the final year of school, specifically to the South of France. I was practically leaping at the idea.

I told my dad about it, explaining that it would be such a great opportunity to learn French. Because Canada is officially a bilingual country, dedicating my time to learning French was a relatively defensible pursuit. Though I'd had it as an elective during boarding school, I argued, this trip would be a completely new opportunity to master it.

Secretly, I thought it would be a great way to have a big adventure. After all, despite the relative fun of boarding school and all its distractions, at my core I still felt a void. I was searching for meaning without any real sense of direction. After hearing me out, my dad decided that traveling to France to study might be a good idea for me.

When it was time to go to the airport, all my family and friends came to see me off. It was the first time I'd be traveling so far from home, and everyone was emotional. People were in tears and hugging me, even my family. I hugged them all back, remaining stoic and but excited.

***

Though I was elated to be going to France with my friends, it turned out to be quite an intense year. The school I went to was Les Canadiennes en France, a co-ed Canadian school. All the Canadian kids were housed with local French families for the purposes of better immersion. Because most of the kids who attended were from private schools in Toronto, going there was costly.

In all, there were about 120 students sent from Canada to France, and as a result of our small numbers and closeness, there were a lot of brotherly and sisterly friendships that formed. The area where we stayed was beautiful and my host family was kind. I lived in a tiny apartment with a roommate and the host parents, who had two young children, so there were six of us crammed into a small space.

In that apartment, my roommate was another Canadian girl who had anorexia and bulimia. Every day after school, she would puzzle me by leaving a pastry on my desk. At the time, I was tall and thin. I could eat whatever I wanted and because I was blessed with a fast metabolism, food never seemed to catch up with me. My roommate left these foods around out of resentment towards me— I guess maybe she wanted to fatten me up.

I'd underestimated how difficult the adjustment would be. The passive-aggressive relationship with my roommate was draining, and the immersion into a very small and cliquey culture was overwhelming. As it turned out, I didn't enjoy my time there as much as I'd thought I would.

I came home at Christmas and cried a lot, asking my parents if I really had to go back. It was my dad who put his foot down. "You taking a year abroad in France is expensive," he said sternly. "You begged me to go and now you're saying you want to come back. You have to finish it, Rachel. You can't keep changing your mind."

After Christmas I returned determined to make the most of it. I lived in Nice and my school was about 30 minutes away in Saint Jean, a beautiful peninsula on the coast. One of my girlfriends at the school, Lana, had a moped, and it was the kind you had to pedal to start the motor going.

I had a Honda dirt bike I rode to school and used to explore the French countryside. We were out on a ride together and we pulled up in front of a bank. "Can you watch my moped for me while I go in?" she asked me. "I'll just be a minute. Make sure nobody steals it!" I said I would, but I wasn't paying close attention—after all, it was just a few minutes.

Sure enough, a young French kid ran up, jumped on the moped and started riding off. I had no idea she hadn't even locked the moped to anything! "*Voleur!*" I shouted to all the people walking by. "*Voleur!*" Even though I was shouting that there was a thief, everyone just looked at me confused. Their faces said it all: *What is that English girl yelling about?*

A moment later, Lana came out and was furious. "I told you to watch it!" she yelled angrily. I didn't know what to say. I apologized profusely, but she blamed me. To make it up to her, I had to drive her back and forth to school for the next couple months while she waited for her insurance claim to settle. It started a rift in our friendship and was a general sign of how things were going in France—it was supposed to be a romantic adventure, but everything kept going wrong.

I wasn't doing well academically because I was so homesick. Jerry and I were dating long-distance and I missed him. Still, I shouldn't have held my breath about him. One day, he called me sadly to say that he'd cheated on me in my absence. I was furious and told him I was done. He protested but I wouldn't hear it—he even flew to France to try to get me to change my mind. I held my ground.

After a while, I filed a complaint with the school about my roommate and got transferred into another apartment. This time, my host was an older French lady and I had no roommate. Things were a bit better, but towards the end of the experience, I was just counting the days until I could go home.

There were some fun times. Later in the year, my friends and I cycled from France to the Italian border, all the way to Venice. Finally, we graduated. At the end of the year, we all went on a big trip to the Greek islands together and stayed in a gorgeous villa, which was a wonderful cap on the entire experience.

The adventure was over. I went to England to visit my grandparents and extended family and then came home. Life went back to normal.

High school had come and gone so fast. Though I was no longer the quiet little girl I had been, my family still had a secret hold on me. It was time to take the next serious life step, and I still didn't know who I was. Regardless, I applied to some colleges and got into Concordia University in Montreal.

Though I was excited, something about it felt disappointing. My father had gone to Oxford for his undergraduate degree and Stanford for his MBA. My brother got his MBA at an elite business school in Massachusetts, and my sister later got her BA at Boston College. Meanwhile, I was going to Concordia University in Montreal, a school that seemed to pale in comparison.

Because I'd already had my big "leaving the nest" moment when I went to France, there was no second goodbye when I went off to college. It was just a continuation of what had already come before. I even decided to major in French, largely because I didn't know what else to do.

While I was truly and completely free for the first time ever, the curriculum at University was harder than I anticipated. The school was in Montreal, and the program consisted of a lot of French speakers with thick French accents going over dense French texts. I found myself dissociating and getting distracted all the time. Unfortunately, the workload didn't permit those kinds of lapses of attention.

After about two years, I knew I shouldn't stay. I decided to transfer closer to home and enrolled in Ryerson University in Toronto.

Throughout the summers in high school and those first two years of college, I'd had various jobs. I continued to model and also worked in some hotels and restaurants. Based on this, I decided to study hospitality and tourism management at Ryerson. Though I was more engaged with that major than I had been with French, I wasn't impressed with the faculty at the school. The teachers in Montreal had been academically serious, but at Ryerson, the hospitality teachers seemed out of touch. I told my dad about my concerns and since he wanted me to succeed, he helped me look into the problem.

After doing a little research, my dad and I decided it might be better for me to apply to the École hôtelière de Lausanne in Switzerland—more famously known as the EHL, for short. The EHL was founded in 1893 and is considered the best hospitality school of its kind in the world. We talked it over and after a year at Ryerson, I applied, thinking the EHL was too exclusive and I'd never be accepted.

When I got in, I was shocked. Now there was a whole new kind of pressure. The plan my dad and I discussed had seemed like a good one, but I wasn't much more sure about tourism and hotels than I'd been about French. I decided to bring it up to my dad as delicately as possible. "I know this school is really expensive," I said, "but I'm not 100 percent sure I want to become a hotel manager. What if I deferred admission and took a year off to work in the industry for a while?"

My dad agreed. As it turned out, I never went.

Chapter 3

The "All-American" Family

Instead of going to the EHL, I started looking for restaurant and hospitality management jobs. I'd already worked as a hostess at Canadian Airlines' private box in Sky Dome, Toronto's baseball stadium, for two summers in a row. It was when the Blue Jays won two World Series' back-to-back in 1992 and 1993. It looked great on a resumé, and I figured it would help me land another job.

Sure enough, I was right. Before long, I got a job helping to open Gretzky's, a Toronto restaurant modeled after the Hard Rock Café—the only difference was the memorabilia was all Wayne Gretzky's. After that, I got another job at a restaurant called Milano, a two-story billiards lounge with a bar. Everything was indigo and there were fish tanks everywhere. It was one of the trendiest places in Toronto at the time.

After gaining some experience, the first really major job I got was for a place called Communique, a communications company that did event and meeting planning.

Through them, I got a gig working for Levi's on contract. I was the account manager and was put in charge of organizing a street-team event to raise awareness for the brand's new product. All the buskers for the event were wearing Levi's jeans and t-shirts.

Through all that, I finally got a full-time job at the W Group, a much bigger Canadian communications company. Though it was a lot of the same work, I was making more money and had more responsibility.

In between jobs, I was still doing some modeling here and there. I signed with a modeling agency on the strength of experience I'd gotten as a teenager. They ended up sending me to Taipei, Taiwan, to model for two months when I was 22.

Taipei was not as exciting as I thought it would be. Though it was supposed to be a two-month contract, I wasn't getting any jobs because my hair was too blonde, and my skin was too tanned. I was confused. They'd seen pictures of me—I'd even had my hair dyed blonder just to go to Taipei. It was all a big miscommunication with my agency.

Another strange thing was that the agency put us up in some subpar lodgings. The place was called the OK Guest Motel, and I learned later that any hotel in Taipei with "OK" in the name is a code word for prostitution. In the rooms next to us, sex workers were coming and going under the cover of night. It was not the glamorous hotel experience we'd been promised. I left after two weeks.

Later, the agency sent me to Tokyo, which lasted for six months. I went for an initial four months, came home in summer, and went back for two more months in the fall. I was a fit model for Issey Miyake, one of the world's most famous designers. I modeled his designs for Paris collections that were due to come out later in spring that year. While I was there, I got all kinds of work. I did jewelry commercials, fashion shows, print ads, catalogues, wedding dresses—you name it.

Being a young model in a big city was an adventure all its own. It was a lifestyle. We were treated like celebrities, and we never paid for our own drinks. Every door was opened for us. In that hedonistic environment, I was constantly faced with choices. A lot of the girls I knew were partying hard and making rash decisions. Though I was excited by it all, I felt a bit like a fish out of water.

Whenever you go somewhere modeling, the agency puts you up with random roommates. People were always coming and going. I once roomed with a stunningly beautiful Scandinavian model and she was hooking up with the guitarist who played in Lenny Kravitz's band. Out of that connection, she invited me to go with her to Lenny Kravitz's concert—she had front row seats.

The concert was at Tokyo Disneyland. After the show, we went backstage where my friend met up with the guitarist. She told me we could get a ride back to the city with them—on their tour bus. On the hour ride back to the hotel, everyone was singing, and I couldn't believe the scene around me. *I'm riding on Lenny Kravitz's tour bus*, I thought as one of his back-up singers sang in my ear.

I kept modeling in Canada for a while as well—I even did a movie in Toronto called *Model by Day* with Famke Janssen. Despite all the wild happenings, most of my choices were relatively conservative. I made good friends with a model from New Zealand who already had a baby. Her house was a stable environment, and whenever she and her husband were at home, everything was quiet and peaceful. Because of that friendship, I never got fully sucked into the modeling world. To get away from the craziness, I would stay with her.

When I got back from Tokyo, Jerry and I picked up dating again. Still, it wasn't as serious. We had a lot of common friends, and it was one of those young adult things. Our re-connection was short-lived—he had a girlfriend while I was away that he never told me about. Ultimately, the whole course of our on-again, off-again relationship ran about six years.

***

I didn't start my next relationship until my mid-twenties. I was at a New Year's Eve party, and I met a super fun and friendly young man named Harry. I was 25 at the time, and he seemed kind—like someone who would treat me well. He warned me at the beginning that he was Jewish, asking if that would be a problem. I told him of course not, but I was being a little naïve. The old patterns with my mum and my boyfriends were still as strong as ever.

I remember one weekend he picked me up at my parents' house to go skiing at his family's chalet in Collingwood, Ontario. To his credit, Harry definitely knew how to work my mum—he was the perfect schmoozer. As we were leaving, he told her what a special girl I was. "Don't worry, I'll take good care of her," he said. My mother looked me up and down. "Well, don't take *too* good care of her," she said. I was horrified.

As we got in the car, it was like I was a little girl again. He hadn't even noticed the comment, but it brought me back to the past. I should've said something to him, but I didn't. Instead, I just stuffed it down. We only dated for about 10 months.

Just as when I was younger, my mum saved all her cruelest comments for *my* boyfriends; she was pretty nice to all my siblings' partners. Through the years, she held onto that special meanness she had for me, which cropped up at all kinds of inappropriate times.

That Christmas, my siblings and myself gathered together in our old home. My mum handed me a present and I opened it in front of everyone. It was a skirt, but it was impossibly short—shorter than anything I would ever choose for myself. My mother was smiling at me expectantly, but I was so uncomfortable.

"Thank you Mum, but it's a bit too short," I said, laughing nervously. I had never said anything to her about any other inappropriate gifts before. It simply wasn't allowed. She tightened her lips and turned her back disapprovingly. I recognized her behavior—I was once again the recipient of "the frosties," as I had nicknamed it in my head.

Later on, my sister shamed me. "I can't believe you would do that!" she said. "That was so rude!" Nobody else could see it. There was a secret power struggle going on, but at the time, only my mum knew she was playing. It only became apparent to me later.

***

Things in my life seemed to be moving along, but that familiar feeling of being stuck and searching for a way out was starting to return. I was 26 and still working at the W Group, often traveling for projects to various places. One of my jobs took me to San Diego, where we were planning an incentive program for a brokerage firm. I brought a videographer with me, and to make things easier, our company hired a bunch of local destination experts because San Diego wasn't a place we knew.

That's where I met Tom.

Tom was one of the experts our company was working with. I first saw him in the lobby of my hotel. We happened to be on-site together at the same time, but we weren't working together directly. Still, our first meeting was a long time coming.

Though we'd never actually crossed paths, my boss kept saying he had someone he wanted to set me up with (namely, Tom). Before that, I'd flown back to Toronto a few times and Tom had actually been in my office working *at my desk*, just by chance. After putting all this together, it started to feel like the Universe was trying to tell me something.

Tom and I hit it off while I was working in San Diego, and I thought he was handsome and charming. I liked the feel of his lifestyle and liked the area as well. When the job was over, we continued dating long distance for a while.

We met in November, and after 10 months, Tom suggested I move to San Diego. By this point, I had fallen for him—and I also knew there was no way I would spend the rest of my life in Canada. After seeing San Diego, something about California was calling to my soul. It seemed totally crazy, but I decided to make a big life change.

I had only just started a career as a meeting and event planner and all my friends were saying I'd lost my mind. I was leaving my family behind, the only family I had in North America. I had just bought a loft in downtown Toronto, my first piece of real estate. I didn't have American citizenship—my nationality status was ambiguous. I had a British passport, but we were only landed immigrants in Canada. To top it all off, I didn't even have a ring on my finger. But none of it mattered.

I got a tenant for the loft downtown and started looking for work in California. My idea was to merge my modeling and planning experience by getting a job as a booking agent. After looking around, I got in touch with a modeling agency in La Jolla.

I had a phone interview that went well and the company said they would be willing to hold a job for me.

"We can help get you a work visa," the man on the phone told me. "You have modeling photos and tear sheets. It'll be easy." With all the arrangements in place, I packed up my little black Volkswagen Jetta and Tom and I left for California. The trip took five days.

The strange part was that Tom's family owned a business in San Diego called The Meeting Planner that essentially did the same thing I was doing in Toronto. To get me in the country legally, he and his family could've easily helped me get a legitimate work visa. That they never did was a little unusual, in retrospect. I asked him about it later in my own quiet way, but there was no real discussion. It was just brushed under the rug.

I never made the connection that I wasn't being fully respected and honored by Tom for leaving my whole life in Toronto behind. As soon as I got there, Tom's family said they needed him to move to Palm Desert to run operations in a new office they were opening. What ultimately happened was I drove across the country and moved in with Tom's uncle in San Diego—along with a brand new, super energetic lab-pit bull mix.

I moved all the way to California, but we were still long-distance. I couldn't go with Tom to Palm Desert; there was no room and there was also no work for me. Instead, I stayed with his uncle and spent a lot of time walking the dog (and taking it to obedience school). Looking back on it, I had such low expectations of life and how to be treated in general. Because of unconscious messages I'd internalized from childhood, I didn't think anybody ought to help me. I didn't think I deserved it. Instead, I was driving out to Palm Desert through the mountains every weekend with the dog in the back of the car to visit him. In the meantime, there weren't many bookings from the modeling agency and I was struggling to make ends meet.

When Tom finally moved back to San Diego three months later, we bought a house and moved to Orange County. I decided to start my own events and management consulting company called Top Tables to make a go of it in another foreign land. I don't know how I did it, but I got hired through my small business as an events consultant for a big firm, managing their in-house tech events. That fall, Tom and I got engaged. I was 27. A year later, we were married. Though it was supposed to be the happiest day of life, it was actually quite a challenge. My parents had just separated after 30 years of marriage and my mother was a complete wreck—she was histrionic.

She intentionally made us late to my rehearsal dinner because she was nervous about seeing my father. Most of my energy that day was focused on the logistics of everything, and making sure my mum was okay. On top of it all, my future mother-in-law didn't say anything about my engagement dress but made a point to compliment my mother's attire. It was an early indicator of the relationship we would have in the future.

***

Tom and I knew from the beginning that we both wanted kids, though it was mostly because it was just the next logical step. There wasn't much discussion about it— it was just what was expected of you as a married adult. We tried for children right away, but for some reason we couldn't get pregnant. I went to see my doctor and got some blood work done.

"How are you feeling?" the doctor asked. I told her I'd been waking up at night all hot and sweaty and wasn't feeling particularly energetic. I definitely wasn't getting pregnant, either.

"Well, we got your blood work back," she said, "and it turns out you're in early menopause."

Though I didn't know what news to expect walking in, it definitely wasn't that. The doctor told me I'd stopped ovulating and that the condition was very unusual for someone so young. Still, she said that with some fertility medication and the possibility of other treatments, I would likely still be able to conceive.

She turned out to be right, because three months later, I was pregnant at 29 years of age. Tom was relatively supportive at the time. He was mostly working normal nine-to-five hours and was around whenever he could be. We did birthing classes together and for a moment, I was hopeful. Life seemed to be okay.

Two weeks before I turned 30, our first daughter, Brynn, was born. Little did I know that getting pregnant once would magically jumpstart my fertility.

When Brynn turned one, we planned a big birthday party for her, and our family came to town to celebrate. The day after the party, my mother and I went out to lunch at Fashion Island in Newport. We both had tuna and after the meal, I shared with my mother I felt nauseous. She said that she did too. Though we assumed it was just bad food, the queasiness stayed with me long after my mother's disappeared. *Oh*, I thought to myself, *I'm familiar with this feeling.*

I went home to take a leftover pregnancy test and sure enough, I was pregnant. I didn't realize that once you take fertility treatments, your entire system can get rebooted. Our second daughter, Mazie, was born just 20 months after Brynn, and my life quickly became a blessed rollercoaster.

***

Having my two girls back-to-back was very demanding. I was constantly breastfeeding and waking up in the middle of the night to take care of them, all while trying to build back my body confidence. Meanwhile, Tom was busy at work and we had no family around to help us out (though my mother would visit every once in a while). We also decided to move to the smaller, nearby beach town of Dana Point.

It was before the age of smartphones, and I had very few friends. Once again, I found myself in a situation that felt just like the one I'd been in as a child—I was trapped at home, isolated from the outside world. Although I'd been so excited to leave Canada and break out on my own, my marriage wasn't going the way I'd hoped it would from the very beginning.

Though there were pockets of joy with the children and our sweet dogs, I was generally quite alone, and fell into a depression. I started taking medication to help but avoided seeing a therapist. I think on some level, I was afraid of what I'd find out about myself. I also started running 25 miles a week. In the meantime, I was having all kinds of friction with my mother-in-law as well. Tom would never take my side. It felt like everything was going wrong and I didn't see a way to fix it.

I soon realized I had become a caged trophy wife.

Tom often travelled for work and always said he was too busy to call. He also seemed disengaged when he was at home. Because he worked in corporate event planning—or party planning, as he called it—the office lifestyle was reminiscent of *Melrose Place*. He was the eternal frat boy, surrounded by beautiful young women. He was getting attention from the girls around him, and it was like he was the office mascot by day. Meanwhile, he was coming home to the reality of a depressed wife and two young and (appropriately) needy children on the nights he was in town and not at client events.

The most hurtful thing was that Tom never seemed to want to spend time with me or just us. The office had a "beer thirty" culture where as soon as the Friday work day was over, everybody would start pouring drinks, and that always seemed to take priority. I'd tried to stay working part time when my daughters were born to stay active and involved in the culture, but it eventually became too much. I had to step away from work.

One time, our family all went to Universal Studios where they had a new ride opening for *The Mummy*. We were all in line on the escalators and Brynn and I were talking about how exciting the ride would be. "I've been here like eight times," Tom said casually. I was stunned. "You've been here eight times?" I asked. He looked at me blankly. "Yeah," he said nonchalantly, "for work events, with clients." Even if there was nothing wrong with that, I didn't know why he'd never told me before.

A gap was growing between us. I felt left out—probably because I was.

I wanted to reconnect and spend more time together and I asked him if he could work from home some Fridays. I suggested that we all rent bikes sometimes and go to the beach on the weekend as a family. But my suggestions would never go anywhere—he would shrug them off or ignore them. He would still go to the beach on the weekends, it was just to go surfing with his friends and girls from the office. There was never any thought of getting a babysitter so I could join him from time to time.

In whatever arguments we would have, he would shame me, shut me out or stonewall me. He was upset we weren't having enough sex, saying we only had it three times a week instead of four or five times a week like his friends and their wives. I didn't know what to say—given everything that was going on, and how little he seemed to be giving to me emotionally, three times a week seemed like quite a lot!

There was a growing feeling that I wasn't good enough, that I couldn't be enough for him. He was making negative comments about my body, our life and me more often. And my desire for him was going away. Our discussions would end with him telling me what to do and walking out of the room. There was rarely any gratitude, and he mostly made unreasonable demands. At the time, I never thought it was all that strange or abnormal. After all, that was what my mother had always done.

He was starting to erode my psyche, and between my depression and his neglect, I felt emotionally and psychologically like I was fighting for my life.

When we had our third anniversary, we went to Cancun and stayed in a beautiful beach resort. Tom wanted to go out bar hopping, whereas I just wanted to relax and be close. Of course, I went out with him anyway. We were in our early 30s, and sitting there at the loud and empty beach bars, all I could think about was how miserable I was. We had two beautiful children back home and here I was, out watching my husband order drinks in bar after bar. It was so not me. It felt like we were drifting apart.

***

Though it feels awful to think about in retrospect, it didn't seem like there were clear markers of things getting worse at the time. I didn't realize how depressed I really was until I was ready to emotionally and mentally crack at any moment.

One morning while Tom was away, I was driving the girls to school and my car broke down. I rang Tom right away and he suggested I call AAA, so I did. The kind tow truck man offered to drop the girls at the school, which was a mile away, and my car went into the shop. I never had a check-in call from Tom the rest of that day. It felt like he really didn't care.

Every summer, the girls and I would go back to Canada, back to the Tip Toes House in the countryside where there was a pool. As things between Tom and I got worse, I would stretch the trips out longer and longer. We once went to Canada for five whole weeks—I was partly doing it to see if Tom would miss us while we were gone. We would talk on the phone periodically, but he only flew out for three or four days in total that summer before going home.

One time I called to check in. "What did you do last night?" I asked. "Oh, I had a party," he replied. *Wait, what?* "You had a party at our house?" I asked again, confused. He replied again that yes, it was at our house. "It was a big party," he said. He hadn't even consulted me. It didn't seem like he missed us at all; he was like a teenager breaking all the rules because his parents were out of town—except he was my 30-something husband.

As the girls got older, I started doing some corporate photography as a side job—just to stay busy and to take my mind off things. Tom and I happened to be working the same event. His company had actually hired me. When it was over, he suggested we all go get a drink next door. When I made my way over, he was already there in the middle of the crowd with his female work colleagues.

I ordered a glass of wine from the bartender and he asked for my ID. I was surprised since I was 35 at the time, and I made a joke about it. "Can you believe they carded me?" I asked rhetorically. "I must look so young!" I joked. "Oh, you're an old hag!" Tom replied. Some people giggled and others went silent. He was the boss, so nobody came to my defense.

I started to suspect Tom was having an affair with someone at his office. There was one day he was working at home that he left his computer open while he was in the shower. His emails were open as well. I snuck over to take a look at some of the correspondence between him and a woman at work. The woman had taken a holiday in Europe to spend time with her own husband, but Tom was emailing her anyway. He kept asking her what he had to do to get her back with him. There were inside jokes, and the entire thing was way more than a little flirtatious. They had even met for a drink after work one day at their "favorite place," unbeknownst to me.

There was another night when he went to the pharmacy and came back with a pack of condoms. He was getting ready for a work trip to Vegas that weekend. "Why did you buy condoms?" I asked him. "They're for us," he said. But I was not going to Las Vegas with him. I thought

I was going crazy and he told me I was overreacting. Out of mental exhaustion, I eventually dropped the subject. Later, when he returned from his trip, I found the same condoms in his overnight bag—and discovered he had a connecting room with one of his female colleagues.

***

I tried to keep busy. We had bought an old fixer-upper of a house, so I did little projects—fixing things, painting. Aside from the photography, I started a side business making miniature kids' chairs that you might see in a Pottery Barn or a similar store. I sold them in some local stores and at little town markets.

I was taking on side projects because I wanted to feel better and do something for myself. I'd tried doing some marketing consulting from home, but having two kids around made the work too stressful. I was isolated, my husband was ignoring me and I had few friends. One of the few outlets I had were the yoga classes I was doing, where I met a friend named Rana. In those yoga sessions, I could breathe through the pain and have some brief relaxation amidst everything else. Still, it felt like nobody in my life could see my pain. My depression was getting so bad that I was having thoughts of suicide.

In that sense, my own affair was something of a perfect storm.

In the midst of all this, there was a man named John who started showing interest in me. He was actually our neighbor. He was friendly with Tom, and they had gone on a bike ride together once. We had each other's phone numbers. He started texting me and giving me the attention I wasn't getting from Tom.

In the back of my mind, all I could think about was Tom's infidelity—I had some evidence that it was happening with one or two women in his office, but he would never admit to anything. He always told me I was wrong when confronted. I was desperate for a lifeline and some kind of real affection. I was spiritually, psychologically and mentally adrift, and it felt like I was slowly drowning.

I didn't know it at the time, but that was the beginning of the end.

In 2008, Tom confronted me about my infidelity. I'd left an email open that had incriminating details about what we'd been doing, and there was no denying it. I was caught red-handed. In no time at all, I was being scapegoated for everything negative that had happened in our marriage. And I took it all on.

A few weeks later, Tom moved out to go stay at a friend's house. We had to tell the girls some of what was happening. He got his own place on Labor Day weekend, and we started trying to do some couple's therapy sessions. Though he stopped going after the first few appointments, I kept going regularly.

I didn't know if it was just a rough patch, or a phase we were going through. Or if it was time to call it quits. For my part, I was ready to work on it. "You have to give him a deadline," my therapist told me. "He can either get in the game or hit the showers."

I told him just that and we were in a holding pattern for a while. My daughters were desperately upset, and everything seemed uncertain. In January, Tom finally came over to the house. He told me our marriage was over, and he walked out. He never admitted to anything he'd done or offered any kind of apology. Our relationship lasted for 10 years.

After we decided to divorce, my mother flew in town to offer some kind of support—though in hindsight, I think she visited to see the "blood on the walls" of my life. One night, my daughters were eating dinner in the kitchen and I had to go to their bedroom to get something. I walked into their shared room and something inside me gave out. I had barely been holding it together, but in that moment, I fell to my knees and sobbed.

I was overwhelmed and felt completely broken. I knew I couldn't go on the way I'd been going, and I was in complete surrender. *What do I do?* I thought miserably between tears. *Someone just tell me what to do, tell me how to fix this.*

Though I didn't know it at the time, what I'd done was a kind of prayer. And it was about to be answered.

***

With the divorce proceedings underway, things got complicated.

At the beginning of that year, Tom and I bought his parents' company on paper, with the hopes that I would get more involved—part-time at first and full-time when the girls were older. Now that our marriage was ending, Tom would have to buy me out of my half of the company. Still, the process of dissolving that arrangement was treacherous.

As per procedure, I hired a forensic accountant to look into the paperwork. What I didn't expect was that he would find nearly a million dollars on paper missing. Tom's parents were helping out with his side of the paperwork, and to this day, I think there was some slight-of-hand that happened during that process—though I couldn't prove it.

Because my mother was still processing her own rough divorce, she was trying to give me all kinds of advice. At the time, my dad was living in Tampa Bay, Florida, and we'd see each other once or twice a year. With my mum, we would visit her in Canada during the summers and most years she would spend the winter months in California to see the girls. In general, she was becoming a bigger presence and influence in my life than she had been in awhile.

"You need to get the best attorney you can," she told me. Her own divorce attorney cost her $200,000 Canadian. "It doesn't matter how much it costs. Hire whoever you need to hire, and I'll help you pay for it." From my side, the attorney I hired told me it might cost another $40,000 to find the missing money from the company buy-out, so I decided to let it go. Taking care of the girls was more important, and I had no extra money lying around to waste.

My plan was to stay in our family home because it was the only home the girls knew. Still, Tom had written in the divorce decree that I had to qualify for a home loan by myself. He wanted to get off the house title if I was to keep it, and he gave me a year to do so.

In the background, the economy was crashing. We had already taken a second mortgage on the home, and I'd had to renegotiate with the bank. Through all that turbulence, I filed for bankruptcy in order to keep the house for as long as I could. As a result, my credit wasn't strong enough to float the mortgage on my own. After a year and a half, Tom legally forced the girls and me out, and we had to sell our house. The girls and I were heartbroken.

We moved into my mum's condo because she said we could, and I didn't know what else to do. The plan was that I'd pay just a small amount of rent and that we would stay for roughly a year while I looked for a new home. Though we'd agreed on everything, she told me after five months that she wanted us out. I asked if we could at least stay until the end of the school year, so the girls wouldn't have to make such a harsh adjustment. She said no.

I should've dragged my feet and said I wouldn't leave. I should've held my ground and said I wasn't going to put my daughters through that. But I didn't. Like the good little girl I was, I said okay, and I moved into a two-bedroom apartment in Dana Point.

Because of my bad post-divorce credit score, I had to pre-pay six months' worth of rent to get in the place. When everything was settled, the bill for the divorce and all the attorneys came due. After that, I called my mum again and told her what the attorney's fees had been. She balked. "I never said I would pay that," my mum said. "I can't help you with that." I was beyond shocked!

I wished she'd dropped that bomb on me before I negotiated the divorce terms. I would've asked for more cash to have on hand. As it was, things were very tight. I had to pay the attorney what I could and tell him I'd pay the rest when I had more money. At the very least, the divorce was over.

No matter how hard the situation was—I had to survive. I had to take care of myself so I could support my darling daughters.

Chapter 4

Finding Jesus

Though things seemed as terrible as they'd ever been, something inside me was shifting.

Ever since that night in my daughters' bedroom, I felt a new openness blossoming inside my heart. I'd been so miserable before and it was all coming from a place of deep self-hatred. I'd been sabotaging myself. The first road I'd been following was my way, the way I thought things had to be. I was ready to try something else.

I started taking my self-care practices more seriously. I committed more fully to yoga and found more peace and growth than I had in the past. I turned a part of my closet in the new apartment into a meditation spot, and was practicing more and more on my own to find inner peace.

As a result of all these practices, strange things started happening.

I was meditating one day in our former family home, when my youngest daughter, Mazie, came in the room. She pointed at a potted tree I had in the corner. "Mummy!" she said, "I see a fairy in the tree!" I opened my eyes to see what she was talking about. "Where do you see it, sweetie?" I asked. "Where is it?" Again, she pointed emphatically at the top of the tree—she was convinced.

Later that night when it was time for bed, I was tucking her in. I went to sit on the edge of her bed and Mazie stopped me. "Mummy, don't sit there!" She yelled. "You're going to sit on Cyrus's soul!" Cyrus was our dog, and he was sleeping on the other side of the bed—but here I was, about to sit on his soul. I moved over a little and finished tucking her in. Just after, she looked at me and cocked her head.

"I see Angels around you, Mummy," she said softly as she closed her eyes. "Everything's going to be okay."

In the meantime, the girls were going back and forth between our new apartment and their dad's place. They were eight and 10 years old. While the youngest was helping me open my mind to a more spiritual way of being, she was also having some of her own challenges. Her emotions and her mood were all over the place, and she was struggling in school. Sometimes she would get so angry she would try to bite and kick me, and I had to send her to her dad's house.

Though it was puzzling, there was nothing ambiguous to me about what Mazie was experiencing. She was seeing and feeling things that were real to her, things I couldn't see. I needed to know what she was going through in those moments. I needed to have access to it.

In a sense, she was becoming my Spirit guide.

***

In 2010, I decided to go to Sedona for a weekend to take a personal spiritual retreat. I figured it could be a treat to myself and a way to center after everything I'd been through with the divorce. One of the practitioners was a Shaman from Canada. He was leading a healing session facilitated inside a beautiful medicine wheel, and he talked about how to expand our hearts and harness our spiritual gifts.

When he sat to work with me, there was something that locked in between us. The energy we shared seemed especially powerful. "You have a special gift," he told me that day. "You have the same gifts I do. You should be using them."

When it was over, I came home exhausted—all the discussion of pain and moving energy took a lot of energy and emotional effort in itself. Typically, when these workshops were over, it was important to get a lot of sleep to integrate the teachings. As soon as I got home in the afternoon, I passed out on the sofa.

Once I started dreaming, I found myself in the same space where I'd fallen asleep. It was a kind of lucid dream; my house was still my house, everything was just a bit different. After getting my bearings, a man with long hair bathed in Light walked up to me. He had a big smile and a calming presence about him. Though it's hard to explain, he was showing me something inside myself, something being pulled from the darkness into the Light.

You have to look in the shadow as well, he seemed to say to me.

And with that, I woke up.

After hearing about my experience, my friend Rana said she had to introduce me to someone she'd been working with. "She's an intuitive and a healer," she said excitedly. "She's amazing! You have to work with her. Her name is Erin." As it turned out, Erin was an instructor from the yoga studio who I already knew! I knew she had a grounded peace within her and an intuitive presence in class, but I had no idea she was a healer as well as a yoga teacher.

In the container of the next two years, I spent plenty of time with Erin developing my spiritual gifts.

After seeing her at the next yoga class, I booked a guided meditation session with her at the yoga studio. As soon as I entered, I felt calm and at peace. We started our guided meditation session together after talking for a few minutes. As soon as Erin started speaking, my eyes felt heavy and I could barely open them. I felt my body become lighter, energy surging through me and seeming to link the two of us together. It was like the rest of the room wasn't even there and I could almost hear a humming in my ears—like an extraordinarily high vibration of energy was moving between us.

When the session was over, we both looked at each other wide-eyed, acknowledging that something special had just happened. It was clear Erin had felt it too, and she said as much. "I think you may have a gift," she said.

I'd been hearing this kind of thing so much that I was starting to believe it myself.

***

Before long, Rana was introducing me to all kinds of other members of her spiritual network. She introduced me to Amy, another alternative healer who focused on energy work and self-forgiveness. We worked together at a workshop in Utah and did phone sessions together (for years, as it turned out).

One day when I was at Rana's house, I saw she had a photo pinned on her whiteboard of a man with long hair and Light beaming around him—the same man who had been in my dream. "Rana, who is that on your whiteboard?" I asked. She smiled and replied, "That's Jesus!"

Rana was a Mormon, so it made sense why she would have a photo of Jesus—still, I was in shock. The familiar iconography of Jesus was not all that familiar to me; after all, my own family hadn't been religious and I hadn't spent any significant amount of time in church. Still, it was the exact same face I'd seen in my dream.

In the beginning of all of the continued sessions with Erin, we would sit together in chairs and talk before settling into meditation. We would wait there together to see what would happen, and she would serve as a channel for a Divine frequency to pass through. Sure enough, something would happen in the room. The energy would change and my body would be magnetized—the energy was so intense that it put me in a trance.

It was all so extraordinary, and I wanted to learn more.

I was branching out into more spiritual practices. Beyond yoga and meditation, I took more workshops and classes and even got certified as a meditation teacher. Though I'd been working as a freelance planning consultant to make money, before long, I decided I would start working with my own clients as an intuitive healer and coach.

In 2011, I got my very first client.

He was a young man in his 20s named Oliver who was referred to me through my chiropractor. He'd been at a party with his friends when they got into a fight with another group of guys. Caught in the tussle, Oliver got punched in the face and fell to the ground hard. He hit his head on concrete and suffered major head trauma. He was in a coma for several days.

Part of my work with him was helping encourage and guide him in his recovery from his head injury. I coached him through meditation for inner peace and to calm the pain. As it turned out, he was also grappling with a marijuana addiction and a lot of existential questions. Though the head injury had been serious, it was also serving as a catalyst for his spiritual awakening, in a strange way.

Still, the biggest shift came later that year, when Rana told me about a ceremony that would be taking place in

Malibu Canyon. "There's a special Shaman in town," she said quietly. "He's a Jewish guy from New York and he's been doing these Ayahuasca tea ceremonies for a very long time. He does incredible work—you have to come."

The conversation took place in late 2011, and at the time, Ayahuasca was hardly something that was in the mainstream. All I knew was that it was a psychedelic tea that opened you up to deep Spirit healing, that it could be an intense experience but that it would be worth it. Still, Rana gave a kind of warning. "The entrance fee is very high," she said. Whatever that meant.

Regardless, I was ready to try it. It was calling me.

***

The ceremony was to be an overnight at this man's house in January 2012. We had to fast all day and to bring our own bedding. We also had to bring some food for everyone to share when it was all over and our own Rubbermaid buckets for the "purging" portion. After that, we also needed water and comfortable clothes.

When the big day came, there was a huge full moon shining over the house. We got there late, so we were packed into the man's living room like sardines, probably 25 of us or more shoulder-to-shoulder. In the front of the house, the Shaman and his assistant were playing music. It all started with the Shaman giving a brief talk about the sacredness of the medicine. After that, he blessed the tea and called us up one by one. As we went up there, each of us would get a blessing, drink the tea and sit back down.

The first thing to notice was that the tea tasted awful—it was like rotting tree bark. That was the first mental game of the night: keep the medicine down. We all went back to our blankets, waiting for it to take effect. The whole room was completely dark except for a dimly lit pathway to the bathroom, and we were all in our own worlds.

After about 20 or 30 minutes, the room started getting hazy and my stomach started aching and cramping as badly as I'd ever felt. My vision went out and I started feeling pain coursing through my body, moving up through my stomach and getting stuck around my solar plexus. All around me, people were writhing and vomiting into buckets. Some people were getting up to go to the bathroom. All of this was the "purging" that we'd expected, the purging of bad energy and trauma that was a part of the experience.

But it wasn't happening for me. I was struggling against it for what felt like hours.

I felt like a ragdoll, hunched over in pain and drooling. I tried to call out to the Shaman for help. After what seemed like an eternity, he finally came over. He seemed annoyed. "What's the problem, Rachel?" he said sternly. I couldn't even speak words—I just pointed at my stomach. After a moment, he put his hands on my head and focused. As he did it, I could feel the energy in my body shifting. It was like there was a knot in the middle of me, and his hands were helping redirect it so the energy could flow again.

I was holding on tight, terrified of losing control, of falling into something greater. He stood beside me and coached me through it, and eventually I was able to purge. But what came next was the last thing I ever expected.

***

I saw myself as a baby, maybe 18 months old. I was lying there, crying by myself, when a dark figure entered my room. It was a man—a family member. He came up to the crib and reached inside and what followed was excruciating pain. He was doing something to the baby— to me.

The pain I felt was unimaginable, like I was dying.

What I was seeing wasn't something the Ayahuasca was making up; it was a memory. A memory I'd repressed since I was a baby, one that was perhaps the basis of all my other memories and identity. Though the Spirit of Ayahuasca, The Grandmother, seemed to be protecting me from the total enormity of it even in that moment, it was clear what I was seeing was sexual abuse. After some moments of this, another energy entered the picture, a young boy who was about five years old emerging in a doorway.

All of a sudden, I was the little boy. I saw him seeing me, seeing the man over me, trying to make sense of it all— confusion, shock, hurt. In that instant, I understood.

The little boy was my brother.

He had accidentally seen this abuse at the hands of our family member when he was only five years old. The horror that he had to witness that washed over me, and with it came a flood of empathy and revelations. In a flash, I felt sure my parents knew it had happened. I also felt my mother's dark heart was present somehow, her closing a door and walking away.

In another flash, I saw how a dark undercurrent of abuse had shaped my relationship with my brother—and my entire family. I saw it unfold in fractal patterns spinning out through our relationships. I saw my father praising my younger sister, the pure and undamaged one in his eyes. I saw my mother turning a blind eye, her shame projecting onto me, turning me into something wretched, something dirty.

But most of all, I felt my brother's confusion.

Rachel, how could you let them do that to you? He asked me. He knew I'd been violated but he didn't understand how or why. He thought I was responsible. He saw what had happened and had learned from it how to treat me. He imitated it. Now I was reliving his punches and kicks, his way of speaking those questions into my body. I felt tears streaming down my face.

In that wash of terror, the plant kept speaking to me.

Do you remember that white cat from your childhood? The one somebody dumped on the side of the country road that came to you?

I replied yes, I did remember, and in an instant, I was back in the Canadian countryside.

Do you remember how he used to claw you?

Again, I replied yes, and as I did, I felt the clawing and scratching all over again.

He was the part of your soul we were returning to you.

I felt the truth of it. This dark part of me, the shadow Jesus warned me about in my dream, had been stalking me my entire life. Even as a nine-year-old child, this cat had been put in my path for my own growth. I'd let him scratch and claw me, trying so hard to earn his trust. I remember being so desperate to befriend him even though he seemed to hate me. And eventually I had.

Do you know why you gave your oldest daughter the middle name Hope?

It was true that Brynn's middle name was Hope, but I hadn't given it much thought before. By this point, I knew the answers were coming regardless if I answered or not.

Names carry energies and frequencies. In that time of your life, when your daughter was to be born, you needed Hope most of all.

***

After all the journeying, people were starting to come out of it. As it was all ending, I was beginning to feel a little better and my pain was subsiding. It felt like all the dominoes of my life had stood up and everything made sense. I understood me for the first time ever. I understood why I hated myself, why I questioned why I was alive, why I was trying to find ways to leave my body.

I had so much self-hate. Though I hadn't known it for most of my life, I always walked around feeling like I was damaged.

I was afraid to look at the people next to me—the entire scene had been so soul-wracking, so intimate. But as I sat up, everything was still dark and shimmering. It was as though I was looking at the room through a screen door. Everyone's image was shaking slightly at the edges, and all the sounds were warped and reverberating. *You're looking at the veil,* a voice said to me. I was terrified but also in awe—this was something I'd been searching for since I was a little girl.

Though there'd been so much pain in my life, I'd always suspected everything I was seeing was just one layer of something much greater. I thought if I tried hard enough, I could break through to the other side. The sensation was going away as quickly as it came, but I realized I was looking at the boundary between the material world and the spiritual world—that the spiritual world was as real as any other. Just as I'd always thought.

The revelation shook me to my core.

My interpretation of that experience was that because the medicine had shown me something so horrifying, it had made up for it by accelerating my spiritual journey. Seeing the veil had been such a gift.

That first experience was eye-opening, but it was also terrifying. I later learned that from a spiritual and astrological perspective, doing Ayahuasca under a full moon on the dawn of a new year in 2012 was a disastrous idea for a first-timer (and perhaps for anybody). The energy of a full moon magnifies and amplifies all the energies that are already there, which partly explains why it was so intense.

I confronted Rana about the experience I'd had, saying she hadn't warned me enough about how severe it might be. Though I'd gotten some insight from it, it had been nearly too intense and not warm or particularly healing as I'd hoped it would be. Even so, she just shrugged it off.

Regardless of that first experience, plant medicine had captured my interest. I'd gotten a glimpse of how powerful and revealing these experiences could be, and I wanted more. I also figured that I'd been through the worst of it already. Surely I'd cleared myself out and any other experiences would be gentler.

As it turned out, I was wrong.

***

Ever since seeing Jesus and having the Ayahuasca experience, my intuitive powers were growing at an accelerated rate. I was getting visions and insights more often.

In one of them, I had a vision of Rana running with wolves during one of our yoga meditations. When I told her about it later, she said that she'd just bought the book *Women Who Run With the Wolves* earlier that day. In another, I was on a call with a girlfriend whose uncle was sick in the hospital. He was so ill that the doctors didn't think he was going to make it.

As I was on the phone with her, I started having a vision. In my mind's eye, I could see her uncle in his hospital bed—and I also saw Jesus entering the room and walking up to him. A moment later, Jesus stretched out his arms and put his hands on my friend's uncle, sending pure Love and Light into his ailing body. I felt the warmth swelling in my body, and I felt a little dizzy. "I think your uncle is going to be okay," I told my friend.

Just a day later, her uncle was released unexpectedly from the hospital—completely healed. The doctors couldn't explain it. Needless to say, I was at a loss for words, and so was my friend.

In the meantime, my own practice continued to grow, and I was feeling more confident as a messenger and healer for others. Through that vision of my friend's uncle, I felt that Jesus was teaching me the power of hands-on healing, that I might be able to channel Light energy into people's bodies through gentle touch during meditation. Though it was something I was still exploring, I was already seeing huge effects from it in my practice, and so were my clients. Some would shake and cry during this process. One client had a spontaneous healing of a chronic uterine pain that none of the most highly regarded doctors in LA could diagnose or cure.

I later took another spiritual workshop in LA where I met a Russian woman named Annika. After we got to know one another, I told her about my first Ayahuasca experience. She was shocked by everything I said. "Rachel, there was no heart in your experience," She said gently. "I work with a man from Peru who uses different plant medicines. His practice is all about opening the heart, and he uses his medicines in that way."

She told me she was going to participate in a movie night and ceremony with this man soon, and asked me to join her. While we were there, they announced a trip to Peru. It would be a two week-long journey through the country, leading to the Amazon jungle, all culminating in some plant work with the Shaman. Though it would cost money and would mean leaving my girls for a little while, there was something about it that called to me.

That first Ayahuasca journey had confirmed for me that there was a higher hand at work in my life. There was a higher intelligence that had orchestrated the things that happened to me, and there were answers to discover. I wanted to know more.

I decided to join the trip as a 40th birthday present to myself.

When the time came, I got on a long plane ride alone and made the journey. I didn't know anyone else who was going. Still, because the spiritual and metaphysical community in California is relatively close-knit, I did know a few of the workshop facilitators who would be down there in the jungle.

The first half of the trip was about appreciating the sights and connecting with the culture and the land. We went through the Sacred Valley in Peru and visited Machu Picchu and Cusco, a breathtaking colonial city in the Andes. After that, we got on another plane and flew to Iquitos, a port in northeastern Peru on the Amazon River. We took a boat up the river, into the heart of the jungle, and arrived by nightfall to our tree house cabins.

The cabins were open to the elements but were walled in with mosquito netting. Though we tried to sleep as best we could, it was an eerie experience. All through the night, the animals in the jungle were screeching away.

There were about 70 people who came to the intensive workshop from all walks of life. People ranged from their 20s to their 60s, though it was mostly people who had already done breathwork, prayer meditation or plant medicine before. Everyone there had already "seen the Light of God," so to speak.

This time around, the experience was three nights of different plant medicines. The first night was Kanna, the second night was Snakeroot and the third night was mushrooms mixed with Ayahuasca baked into a chocolate. As it turned out, that combination is relatively rare and is something of a secret recipe—it also made the experience a little gentler but still very deep.

Once again, the plant was showing me things I'd forgotten or repressed.

I was taken back to when I was a child, when what kept me going were my childhood pets. They had been my best friends. I remembered my mule, Jenny. I could see our old paddock we shared with Lee.

In the middle of my journey, my heart was burst open and I was taken to a place where I saw Jenny walking on the shoulder of a country road, near my childhood home—but I knew she'd died years before. I asked Jenny what happened to her and she told me a truck had hit her. "I was coming to find you," she said. "I always knew you'd been abused. I wanted to find you and protect you." My heart wept with Love and Gratitude for her.

I realized that what had been happening in my home life was reflected in what happened to my pets as well. Many of them had met their ends through my mother's neglect. Once, she let our cats out after specifically being asked not to and my siblings and I never saw them again. We assumed they met their fate with the coyotes. I suspected the same thing happened to my rabbit Tootsu.

I remembered the day I came home asking about my rabbit and my mother said she didn't know what happened, that Tootsu ran away. Though I was heartbroken, I couldn't cry. I completely dissociated. But the memories were coming back—some years later, our gardeners came to the door. They mentioned a rabbit they'd found trapped under the house years before.

When I asked them about it they looked confused. "She didn't tell you?" they asked. "Tootsu got trapped under the house and couldn't get out." When the gardeners found her skeleton, there were signs that she tried to burrow out from under the house. She'd been trying to climb out for hours.

My other rabbit Flopsy was an Angora, and needed constant grooming or she'd choke on her own hair. When I left for boarding school, my mother promised she would do it. But she never did and Flopsy got wool-block. Her stomach filled up with her own wool, causing loss of appetite and eventually life-ending dehydration.

All the memories were coming back, all these child-hood friends I'd lost at the hands of my mother. The plant was showing me I'd repressed so many of my painful childhood memories. The healing came in remembering how much warmth and Love I'd felt with my pets, how much they saw me, felt me and truly wanted to protect me. They were so intuitive.

But the worst revelations were yet to come.

Before long, I was being shown something else. It felt like it was starting when I was 10 years old. I saw my memories unspooling like a filmstrip, though there were frames missing. In one of the moments, I saw a super-market in Canada we used to shop at and was immediately filled with dread.

The plant showed me standing in front of a big metal delivery container. It was a steel box like the ones they take off the back of a truck, one with a big sliding metal door.

I felt unsafe and flushed with panic. *Where's my sister?* I thought. The plant showed me my sister and brother, safe inside the supermarket with my mother. *But why am*

I out back by myself? A moment later, the door was opening and a dark presence—an adult man—was ushering me inside the container. As the door slid shut, I was plunged into pain and terror once again, just like before.

Just like when I was only 18 months old.

I then got a flash from walking through the supermarket with a sore, scratchy throat. *I'm allergic to peanuts*, I thought. *I ate a peanut.* The words were repeating through my head on a loop, over and over again, each time ringing more and more hollow. As the dots connected in my mind, all I could see were the dark insides of the shipping container.

At that, the filmstrip of my life swept back and I could see other strips, other collections of memories with similar holes in them.

I saw my mother standing in some of them nervously, speaking to men who were strangers, money changing hands—into her hands. Once again, the horror that these were my memories blanched me like cold water. Another flash of images: my mother's high-end wardrobe full of clothes and shoes, her new car and expensive jewelry.

I had been sold for sex. It had happened too many times to count.

Once again, though it was shocking and terrifying to revisit, I was being protected from the entirety of the experiences. I remembered what the Shaman said to us, "Just because you are visiting Hell doesn't mean you have to sight-see."

I was crying and shaking. I plunged into my mother's mind and felt her jealousy, her spite whenever my father would pay any attention to me. Her cruel comments to boyfriends, the lingerie. *You're the one who's sexy*, I could feel her say. *No wonder men want you.*

Why? I thought helplessly, in disbelief. *Why would she do that?*

There were layers. The need for material things was one; hidden money issues were another layer. Another was the dark need to project onto me, some hatred for me that she had to justify however she could. There were deeper and darker layers beyond that, things I was too afraid to move into and still can't speak about.

At the bottom of it was one strange, contradictory statement coming from her: *they chose Rachel over me.*

***

Once again, the plant had showed me things I'd never known. Again it had been horrifying, but this time, it had also been more manageable. More pieces fell into place, and ultimately, I was grateful.

Everything was becoming clear now. However awful it was, I had found pieces of myself that had been hidden or lost from me for so long. I was reconnecting with myself, a part that I thought was long gone. And there was still a chance for me.

I'd been sexually violated for years, and that fact explained so much. It was a shadow that had been brought into the Light.

I was so little, and my most sacred boundaries had been crossed over and over again. Bad behaviors had been imprinted onto my body and my Spirit. Out of that programming, I'd confused sex for Love. I had no sense of what loyalty felt like. I thought so little of myself, but I didn't have to anymore. I'd found the strength to say no to my brother's friends when I was 12, and I could keep tapping into that same strength again and again.

From that trip to Peru, my biggest takeaway the Shamans left me with was that everything in life is relational. How we relate to substances, our hearts, to others, to Life, to food, to Spirit. All of it is relational and in flux. And relationships can be changed and repaired.

After I came back from Peru, I made plant medicine a regular part of my life, participating in it about once every three to four months. I was meditating more and all the experiences I had were beginning to integrate. I remember having a visual epiphany once during meditation of all the places in my brain where psychological trauma had been physically stored. It was like there were electrical scars on some points, some places where the circuitry was broken.

In another meditation, I was looking into a mirror and meditating on my third eye. As I breathed in and out, I noticed my reflection had become headless. I was shocked, but I kept breathing through it. After that, my head came back, but it was all pixelated—and I could see the spaces between the pixels, like I was seeing through to an etheric self.

Still breathing, my face transformed into a future, 80-year-old version of myself with wrinkles and grey hair. *I look pretty good for 80 years old*, I thought with a chuckle. As I breathed, my face kept morphing back and forth between images, of people I once knew and faces I'd never seen before. At the end of it all, I became headless again.

What appeared at the end was Jesus's face superimposed over my face. He was smiling at me.

As it turns out, that shapeshifting experience I had is not uncommon among Shamans. The theory is that once a person has taken a powerful plant medicine, that plant's Spirit or frequency is forever encoded in their Being. Because of that, those people can quiet their minds and open to the Spirit, sometimes inadvertently summoning those plant Spirits back.

On the other hand, you can also call them back willingly—if you're experienced enough.

Chapter 5

Gabriel and the Tree of Life

The summer after coming back from Peru, I went to another ceremony in Malibu where I met a wandering Shaman. He was from Mexico, and he'd come to do the plant medicine ceremony as well. He played the didgeridoo and that first night we stayed up all night together, laughing and talking about everything we'd experienced. He was an intuitive healer as well, and he recognized the same gifts in me. Our birthdays were one day apart, but in different years.

His name was Gabriel.

We had an immediate connection and when the weekend was over, we exchanged information and kept in touch. He lived in Ojai, but we dated and visited one another for a while. Gabriel was a free spirit, someone with a pure heart and a wide-open consciousness—someone who had been seeking answers his whole life, just like me. I had a deeper connection with him than I'd ever felt with anyone.

After we'd been dating for a while, Gabriel came from Ojai to Orange County so that we could be together and moved in with my two daughters and me. Around the same time, I felt a yearning and started having clear dreams about opening a meditation studio. After discussing it, Gabriel and I decided to open a studio in Orange County, split the business fifty-fifty and work with clients together.

Though the paperwork was done in 2012, we officially opened The Tree of Life in 2013, in a building shared by several outpatient addiction recovery programs. I taught spiritual fitness classes, coached clients one-on-one and added new clients who were looking to use meditation and spiritual recovery to support them overcoming their drug and alcohol addictions.

As soon as The Tree of Life opened, Jesus became even more of a full-time character in my life.

While I was teaching in the new space, he would appear to me in the room and his energy would feel very intense. Many of my clients who felt connected to him would feel his presence as well. Though not everybody could see what I saw, Jesus would gesture to me throughout the teachings while I led classes. He would sometimes tell me to ask them things.

"How do you feel about Jesus?" I would ask the class. Sometimes people would be puzzled; other times, they would react warmly. All the while, Jesus would smile at me. As we sat down for meditation, Jesus gave me more guidance on how to help the clients. Again, he stressed the importance of hands-on healing.

Put your hands on their feet, he would tell me.

Everyone would lie down and meditate, and just as I'd been told, I would carefully put my palms on the soles of my clients' feet. With their permission, I focused on sending out a healing frequency, on channeling Divine Love into each of them. In many cases, people would start shaking and crying.

Everyone had visceral physical responses to the experience—some of the people were strong, stoic men who hadn't cried in years. Even though some of the clients were in detox, had dirty feet or didn't have the best hygiene, I still did as Jesus said. It was directly following in his footsteps; after all, he also spent much time dedicated to washing the feet of "sinners."

As the practice grew, I felt my spiritual abilities getting stronger and my heart opening more and more. Though Gabriel was incredibly emotionally supportive, it became clear pretty quickly that he wasn't as supportive from a business standpoint. Though he would come to The Tree of Life to play music and do monthly workshops, he would often go off traveling and sharing his healing music with the world as well.

In the meantime, I spent more and more time meditating on my trauma and childhood pain, trying to integrate the wisdom I'd gotten. What I'd come to realize was that everything I'd gone through at a young age had not been pointless pain and suffering.

It had been my initiation as a healer.

I began to say to myself the same things I was telling my clients struggling with addiction: Even in that deepest darkness, there was a silver lining—those experiences made us organic seekers of something greater than ourselves. And that was a beautiful, beautiful thing.

It reminded me of the metaphor of the lotus flower, which is so important to spirituality. It grows out of mud. The deeper the initiation, the more beautiful the flower. The more my clients and I could do deep inner dives into our own personal mud, the more beautiful our lives would ultimately become.

As above, so below.

***

Gabriel and I were together for two and a half years and they were some of the most beautiful and healing of my life. Still, it was becoming clear that Gabriel might not be someone I could settle down with. He never wanted to stay in one place; he wanted to roam free. He was truly happiest being a wandering Shaman. I could feel a change on the horizon for us and I needed more support with The Tree of Life and raising the girls. On top of that, despite all the boundary breaks the plant medicine had shown me, my relationship with my mother was still an unsettled question.

Something was in the air.

In 2015, a strange thing happened. My mother was in town visiting. I'd brought her down to The Tree of

Life to have a sound healing experience of her own. She was behind the door in one of the studio's rooms when in walked a yogi, dressed in long sage-colored robes. The yogi was an Indian man with a thick accent who greeted me with a big smile.

"God sent me here today," he told me. Even in my line of work, this was unusual. "I can feel this is where I am supposed to be. I have some things to tell you." I supposed he was just a wandering teacher, and that our interaction was some kind of synchronicity. Inside, I smiled. He was highly intuitive just like me! As such, he was telling me things about myself and about the future—things I already knew.

But what he said at the end shook me back to reality.

"There is a woman," he said, "who has a very dark heart for you. It is not good for you and your family. You need to stay away from her." As he said it, I got chills. At the same time, it felt like I could see my mother listening and watching from behind the closed door in the back. I could feel malicious energy seeping through the door and into the studio, looking for me to wrap around.

Evil is such a strong word, so the way the yogi put it to me that day made more sense. There was some deeper dark force at work between my mother and I, something that went beyond just a regular relationship. The horrible things my mother had done to me over the years truly didn't make sense on any rational level—there was no need for her to be so cruel, ever.

And yet here I was, still trying to patch over all the old darkness. Still trying to mend something that might not be mendable.

***

As I'd suspected, Gabriel and I soon had a conversation about needing to part ways. He longed for more adventure and to get back out into the world. Though we loved each other deeply and were connected on a soul level, we both knew it was for the best. He moved out and we still saw each other occasionally. It was very difficult.

We saw each other here and there, for a meal or a movie. I gave us some space and after some time had passed, we started talking about reconciling. I asked him to meet the girls and I for dinner one day. During our meal together, he told me he was planning to go to Egypt for a spiritual pilgrimage with his mother and some of her friends.

"Oh," I said, "maybe I could go too?" He nodded and smiled. But just then, I heard a voice of wisdom speak to me: *No, you can't.* "Actually, I can't," I said quickly. "I have the girls and the studio to look after."

A few weeks later, he asked to meet with me alone. Though it was good to see him, I noticed something as soon as I sat down. While his face was clean, I could energetically see lipstick all over his face. "Who's the other woman?" I asked him. He seemed shocked that my intuition was so sharp and he acted very embarrassed.

"I've started seeing someone else," he said. My heart dropped. I still had strong feelings for him and I thought there was a chance we'd be getting back together. As it turned out, he'd already started to move on. It was clear our separation wouldn't be temporary. In my heart, it felt like he'd cheated. He'd been living in my mother's condo for a few months and we'd still been tied together in that way. Now, we were unraveling for good.

A month later, we had our heart-wrenching goodbye. I wept as he placed my hand on his cheek. It all felt so final, and part of me was unsure if I would ever see him again.

Soon after in August, I went on a trip to Mexico with my father and my daughters. The reality that Gabriel and I had parted was just sinking in, and my grief was extraordinary. I was completely flattened by it, and I couldn't stop crying. I'd been working with a coach at the time that said it was a positive sign. "Your heart has grown so big," he said. But I knew that wasn't it. Although Gabriel and I were deeply connected, it didn't make sense that my grief was so all encompassing. I couldn't understand it.

I suddenly felt fear. I couldn't tell where it was coming from or pointing towards, but it was a fear around Gabriel. We were by Lake Chapala, Mexico on vacation, and I called Gabriel's mother. "He can't go to Egypt," I blurted into the phone. His mother was confused. Because Gabriel and I had dated for so long, she knew me well and she knew we were going through a separation. As such, she was caring and sympathetic. She responded to me in broken English.

"Gabriel still go Egypt," she said gently. "I love you, love you." She must have said this about 20 times.

Gabriel and his mother went on the trip in September. I was in Toronto at the time visiting my sister, brother-in-law, nephews and nieces. The night before my return to California, I had a dream. In the dream, Gabriel walked up to me and hugged me, squeezing so tightly. After that, he broke the hug and started walking away. I reached out and put my hand on his naked back. I could feel the warmth of his skin under my fingers, but he just kept walking. I woke up thinking it felt so surreal and strange.

About six hours later, I was at my nephew's soccer game and a storm front rolled in. It started pouring rain. I was quite shivery and my nails were turning blue. Next thing I knew, I was crying. *Rachel, what is wrong with you?* I thought. Though I was cold, it definitely wasn't *that* cold—and I had no real reason to be so upset. Still, my body and heart were telling me something.

I was set to fly back to California later that afternoon. As I got on the plane, I tried to close my eyes and get some rest. Behind my eyelids, all I could see was an image of Gabriel and his new girlfriend standing together. I could see them right in front of me, clear as day. The image wouldn't go away. I was restless the entire flight and couldn't sleep, and usually I can't stay awake on planes. When I finally landed at LAX, I turned my phone back on and saw I had a message.

It was from Gabriel's sister, Rosa. It was 1:30 in the morning. I called her back.

"I have terrible news," she said over the phone. I was still in the car on the way home. "Why don't you call me back when you're home and we'll talk." It was already so late that I told her I didn't want to wait. "Just tell me what it is now," I said. Rosa took a deep breath.

"Gabriel is dead."

I couldn't believe my ears. There was a delayed long-distance echo over the phone, so I asked her to repeat it. "Gabriel is dead," she said again. I didn't understand how it was possible.

I called my friend Annika in shock and woke her up with the news. "There must be some mistake," she assured me. She checked Gabriel's Facebook page and the condolence posts were already coming in. "He posted one picture from his trip," she told me quietly. It was a picture of him and his new girlfriend, along with two other women. I was speechless. It was another blow to my heart.

Rosa later told me that Gabriel had been traveling with their mother and others in convoy through the White Desert in Egypt. There were about 20 people with them, all guides and other people on the pilgrimage.

Though they'd been officially allowed permission from the government to travel there, part way through the trip, an Egyptian Apache military helicopter had appeared out of nowhere and took aim at them. It opened fire on their jeeps. Though the gunfire had annihilated some of the vehicles right away, others tried to veer off, to avoid the artillery shells.

We later learned they were under attack for three to four hours.

The event made international news. Out of the 20 people who were on the trip, 16 were killed. Gabriel's mother was injured, but she survived. His girlfriend had lived as well. Although she was an American, the news was reporting that the people in the convoy were all Mexican nationals traveling through the desert that were fired on by mistake. Nobody wanted the news out that there'd been an American with the group. It was a cover-up.

I went to bed in complete despair that night, in disbelief. The grief I felt in Mexico wasn't just mourning for the end of our relationship. I was mourning Gabriel's death before it even happened. I felt like a part of me had died too. After tossing and turning for a while, I finally fell asleep.

I woke up again at 4am to a breeze blowing through my bedroom window. I was still in the home Gabriel and I had shared, and I felt his presence. *He's here*, I thought. I immediately knew it. I opened my eyes and right in my bedroom, there was Gabriel. He appeared to me, bright white, as a vision at the foot of my bed, all dressed in his ornate, Huichol indigenous clothing, complete with embroidery. It was the same outfit he wore for all of his ceremonies.

After a moment, he beckoned from the foot of my bed. "Come with me," he said.

In Spirit, he pulled me out of bed and through the window, out to look at the hills behind our house. "Do you see all this?" he asked. I said I did. "This is the veil," he said. "This is the illusion. Come with me to the other side." Though I was looking at an entire landscape, Gabriel lifted his hand out and under it somehow, pulling it up like it was a thick stage curtain. It was like all the world's scenery was painted on top of this velvety fabric.

As we crouched and walked underneath it, I was in awe. We were standing in the middle of an infinite field of pure white Light. I couldn't see any boundaries or horizons, and it was nearly blinding, truly. Gabriel moved me through the space as an enormous and beautiful tree appeared before us. It towered above us and the bark was a color I had never seen before—a kind of rich, living red.

We got closer and closer to the tree and Gabriel guided me to look at the flowers growing on its trunk. I did, and each one looked like a little cherry blossom made of the finest tissue paper. The flowers seemed lit from the inside by fairy lights—it was the Light of pure Spirit shining through everything. Seeing it up close literally took my breath away.

I looked up at the tree and the bark, which seemed somehow to be breathing. "This is the Tree of Life, isn't it?" I asked him. He nodded.

We walked around to the other side of the tree and there was a bench carved into the front. We sat together on the bench for a long time, in silence. Even though our story had been cut short, Gabriel came back to give me this as a gift of pure Love. My entire life, I'd been looking for the Truth of what was beyond the veil. Though I'd dived deep into myself and had seen and felt the veil once before, I'd never truly seen beyond it in this way.

Now here I was, looking directly at the Source of it all. This other reality made sense. I'm not sure how long the vision lasted, but I know we sat for a long, long time. In our hearts we both knew it would be the only time we would ever have this experience together. The peaceful stillness was so calming and serene.

Perhaps for the first time ever I knew, deep in my soul, that Life was much more mystical than I ever could have imagined.

Chapter 6

Aftermath

When Gabriel died, his body was flown back to Mexico. I never got to go to the memorial or a funeral. I did a soft ceremony for him at Tree of Life, because many people asked me to. People needed something to honor him. So many people around the world had been touched by him, and many others celebrated Gabriel at their own private gatherings as well.

My connection with Jesus had already been established before Gabriel entered the picture, but it had been Gabriel who'd really helped me embrace it. He'd even showed up at my house one day with a giant painting of Jesus in his hands, smiling. He knew I felt a special connection there, and he helped me lean into it. It was deeply honoring and validating.

I was talking to my brother about what happened to Gabriel and his words shook me. "Rachel, he was murdered," he said. I had never felt the enormity of that fact before, but it was true. Gabriel had been terrorized and murdered. It was another layer of grief to go through, but it was also a necessary one. I went into a deeper place of feeling the Truth of that torment and hurt.

I was still running Tree of Life when Gabriel was killed, but things were feeling unsustainable. I was taking myself and my daughters through the grief journey, seeing 40 to 60 clients a week alone and being harangued by reporters, not to mention a private eye that was stalking me outside my studio, hired by Gabriel's family and a friend looking for I-don't-know-what exactly. They kept asking about my connections to Gabriel and what had happened in Egypt. I was beyond drained.

***

Several months later, I meditated on what to do about the studio one night, asking Jesus for guidance in particular. The two recovery centers in our building had moved out, and it was unclear where our clients would be coming from in the future. *Close the studio*, a voice came back to me. Although it had been a ton of work to get it off the ground, I knew it was a chapter in my life that was ending. I did what I was told, closed the studio and moved out of the house that the girls and I had shared with Gabriel. It was too emotionally difficult and too expensive to stay there.

Just five days after Gabriel's death or transition, I took Ayahuasca and had a profound and moving vision where I witnessed and experienced Gabriel's ascension.

In the vision, I saw his body rising up through blue and white hoops of Light. As he ascended, I could see and feel his human foibles and insecurities shedding from his Spirit body. All his feelings of anger, shame, sadness and jealousy were being stripped away.

His physical body was being illuminated into a body of pure Light. It was breathtaking.

Because we were still spiritually connected, it was like I was feeling everything he was feeling. For a moment, I was weightless; we were both being released of our constrictions. As Gabriel passed through the final hoop he disappeared into pure white Light. God's Light. I have never felt so open and free before in my life. It was like spiritual ecstasy. And then I was filled with a gentle and naïve envy unlike any I'd ever known.

Gabriel had achieved total spiritual freedom, and I was still here, with more work to do.

For him, there would be no more responsibilities and no more pain. I had tasted in my own nervous system what it would be like to feel that. I'd glimpsed it, and I knew it was possible. *Take me, too!* I could feel how real "this place" was. Part of me wanted to go.

Coming out of it, I felt I had a new clarity and direction.

As spiritual teachers, so much of what we teach and transmit is what we can pass through our nervous systems and energy fields. When we have unique experiences, each has its own vibration or frequency that in essence gets coded into us. It gets imprinted in our systems and is there with us, forever. The experience of watching Gabriel was like that. And knowing him in life was like that, too.

***

About six months after Gabriel died, I wrote a serious letter to my mother. I didn't do it out of a place of malice or hate; I did it to set a boundary. It was a sacred boundary she'd crossed so many times years ago, one I wanted to restore. I just wanted her to know I remembered. That I knew what she did to me, and that she could no longer buy my silence, no matter how many millions of dollars she had and held over me. My voice was no longer for sale.

She never responded to my letter, which felt like an admission of guilt. What she did do, however, was to make copies of the letter and distribute it to my entire family. She never replied to me personally. I haven't spoken to her since. It has now been nearly four years.

My sister began distancing herself from me as a result of the letter, and my brother was angry and upset. My father made reference to it once, but he never went into detail or explained his position. Swept-under-rug was his modus operandi. Everyone had his or her own version of denial after I'd told my truth. But I understood. Facing shadows isn't for everybody—it's hard work. I accepted the situation for what it was. Before I wrote the letter, I'd been going into another heavy and deep depression. After I sent it, the depression lifted.

About a year after sending the letter to my mother, I heard my ex-husband Tom got married in Las Vegas. Although we'd grown distant over the years, that pain became brand new again when I heard the news. After closing my studio, I was feeling a bit unsettled and listless. In the middle of a meditation, Jesus came to me once again. In the vision, he placed a purple heart on my clothing. In that moment, I felt seen, loved and understood. He was still walking beside me, telling me how courageous I was.

Although Tom's remarriage still hurt, I summoned all the inner strength and Grace I could. Through the pain, I could still feel a gentle glow inside me. One of my friends must've noticed how equanimous I seemed in light of it all, and she commented on it one day. "Rachel, you always handle everything with so much grace," she said. "I know it will all get reflected back to you." I knew she was right. My vision of Jesus with the purple heart seemed to confirm it. After a lifetime of seeking, I understood that we were all put here to help each other evolve, and to guide and walk each other back home.

In 2016, I went on a second trip to Peru, into the Andes. The Shamans I saw there used Huachuma, a lesser-known plant medicine. Where Ayahuasca is usually referred to as The Divine Grandmother, Huachuma is The Divine Grandfather. As with Ayahuasca, these Spirit journeys usually encourage self-reflection and quiet rather than talking with others. Still, as people were beginning to come out of it at the end, we started to speak with one another.

I was with Dennis, a former client and now friend who worked in scientific publishing and lived in Peru. Some time had passed, and I'd been trying to open my heart to other men again. "Rachel," he asked me, "whatever happened with Peter?" Peter had been a male confidant of mine I'd told Dennis about. He was someone I thought I might make a deeper bond with, though it hadn't turned romantic.

Though the medicine was beginning to wear off, I felt a surge of energy in that moment as something was revealed to me. A voice was reaffirming what I already knew, that what Peter and I had shared was special and to be treasured. We had what I felt was a special connection that never deepened beyond friendship.

The first feeling I experienced was the grief once more, though it quickly gave way into acceptance and then into wonder. The idea that Peter and I had not stepped into our "soul contract" with one another was revealed to me. It suddenly seemed clear that this must be so: a Power greater than us had orchestrated or planned that our souls would meet and remember each other.

But by the same token, I suddenly saw that there were *other* soul contracts floating out there for me in the beyond—and that I hadn't fulfilled some of them! Though I couldn't pinpoint who these unfulfilled energies connected to, I knew that for some of them, it was too late. There was a recent opportunity for a deep soul connection the Universe had laid out before me, that the other person hadn't stepped into. The medicine guided me into deep Gratitude for the connection I had made with my friend, but it also helped me sink into mourning for this other Divinely ordained connection I had missed. Even so, I sensed that there were still open soul contracts out there waiting for me—there was still much more ahead.

It was an unexpected revelation, but it brought me a peace and clarity. The idea of a soulmate is a powerful and compelling one, but it also can seem a little final. What happens if you only have one soulmate and you miss them in life? Or they die before you do? The Truth is that we do have *many* possible soulmates and soul contracts, and not all of them get fulfilled because of our own free will. Even so, the Universe provides these paths into Love for us to find.

Ultimately, everyone is entitled to follow his or her own path. And on each one, we carry in our hearts the pilot Light of Christ consciousness and Jesus's Love. just as with Jesus, we can choose to honor those contracts if we want to. We can choose to sit down at the table. In a sense, I feel, we all have an open soul contract with Jesus.

Still, it's at these most crucial and meaningful moments that words fail. We can step into Love with others and with Jesus, but there's still another way to say it. In essence, when we step into Jesus's Love, we step into our own hearts. The ultimate soul contract, then, is the one we have with ourselves.

Part Two

Chapter 7

Opening to the Divine

Isn't it time we took Jesus off the cross?

This was an insight and a question that came to me during meditation and in the writing of this book. In most people's minds, Jesus is synonymous with crucifixion. In many images and representations of Him, he's seen up on the cross, suffering for the sins of humanity. It's an image that shocks us into awareness, and it was meant to—that was Jesus's intention! Still, Jesus's message was one of Divine Love, and it's that message that has nearly been lost.

Though I've been on a serious journey and have definitely transcended my former self, the price I paid has been huge. I had to rewire my entire nervous system, to change all my thoughts and beliefs and overcome PTSD and CPTSD. Today, I am still a work in progress, and I don't claim to be enlightened. Turning to plant medicine for insights and answers was a risky choice, particularly while I was raising two young girls.

In all, the path I chose was a high-risk path. I'm fortunate it has led me to where I am.

An idea that gets debated a lot in spiritual communities is that "we chose this on a soul level." This means before we were materially here, our souls were calling out for the exact path we ended up living. Our Higher Self somehow orchestrated with our Higher Power to choose our experiences. But of course, nobody remembers choosing.

I'm not sure I like the framing of that. For me, this idea brings a subtle energy of guilt.

When bad things happen to us, we might ask: *Why would I do this to myself? Why would I choose this?* One of my teachers, Matt Khan, has offered another way to turn the energy of that idea around. Perhaps we didn't choose these hard experiences; perhaps we were *chosen* for them.

We all have a natural curiosity about what we're doing here on Earth. It's common among all people, but for me, it was a summoning. My whole life, I felt I was being called to a deeper truth, to a deeper reason for being. I didn't know at the beginning that I was being called by a being I identify as Jesus. As soon as I answered that call, my life changed, and miracles beyond being a mum started happening. I started being able to feel the miracle of myself.

It's easy to get distracted by language, systems of thought and ideology. But ultimately, it's not about the words. It's about the things behind the words, and it's about belief.

There's a strong doctrine within the Christian church that Jesus *belongs to* the church. But how do we really know that? When we start to question that, we can get to some interesting places. What if Jesus was truly "just a man" with incredible teachings to share? After all, the story of Jesus as we know it was only shared hundreds of years after he'd died, when someone rolled it all together into a religion. What was the real intention behind it all?

Today, religion has been tainted. It's been rightfully identified as a patriarchal structure. It's a structure that found a powerful and true source and built a complex system around it. A system with rank and order, using emotions like shame and guilt to accrue power and to control how people behave. But that was never what Jesus wanted. The god of a religion like that ought to be written with a small g—to me, it's not the real God.

Even for those who aren't religious, the judgment and the shame are so strong that they are now in the collective. Even people who weren't raised in the church are imprinted with some of the church's pain and values.

Although Jesus is far more loving than the church might have us believe, the truth is still more complicated. In his stories, Jesus was known to "go rogue" occasionally as well. For more evidence, just consider the Biblical story of Jesus entering the Temple and driving out all the people buying and selling animals for sacrifice. He knocks over the tables of the money changers and the chairs of those selling doves.

Though the doctrine of "turn the other cheek" is prevalent, it sometimes gets taken out of context. For Jesus, "turning the other cheek" didn't mean letting people walk all over him. It was more complex than that.

To him, it meant honoring and loving everything all at once and accepting it without resistance or undue aggression—including all of the contradictions that he couldn't resolve. It was a radical, non-dualistic view of abiding Love. In Jesus's own story, he struggled with his darkness and his own shadow. In turn, he encourages us to find where we are shrouded in our own hearts and bring those parts into the Light.

Jesus's own faith in God's Divine Love was repeatedly tested. Another way to say that is what was being tested was his own Love for himself.

In that regard, we're really no different than Jesus. Each of us has our own shadow, our own story and path to walk. Sharing our stories can inspire people, and maybe help some people take a turn in their lives. It can open people up. In the process of telling our own stories together, we start to create touchstones that can serve as markers on the spiritual path.

For me, those markers were yoga, meditation, spiritual teachings, plant medicine and my daughters' Love. For others, the touchstones could be completely different. The Truth beneath it all is that a Higher Power is always there, sitting across the table from us, with an extra chair pulled out. We can surrender and sit in the chair at any time; a Higher Power will never force us but will always nudge us.

We do have to choose to sit down on our own.

The Universe is very chatty, but we have to be quiet to hear what it's saying. There's an entire world outside us that responds to our beliefs, our level of awareness and our unique consciousness. Our brains try to compartmentalize and understand it all too much. The key to spirituality and a path to Jesus is to accept and Love it all at once without judgment.

And after that, you can still just laugh and say, "I don't know, let's go get some ice cream." After all, the Dalai Lama says if you want enlightenment, lighten up. It's not Buddhism or Shamanism or Islam or Christianity. They're all part of the "31 flavors" of spirituality (one of my favorite teachings).

They're all attempted and true paths to the one spiritual Truth. In my understanding, it's all the same as Jesus. That is the Christ Consciousness.

I attended the Self-Realization Fellowship's Temple in Encinitas, where the founder Paramahansa Yogananda created the most beautiful meditation gardens on the cliffside. It is a Hindu temple, and on their altar, they have all these photos of ascended gurus. Among them was a picture of Jesus—and I thought that was beautiful. As I meditated on the open-heartedness and completeness of that image, I got a vision. One of the gurus appeared to me.

I have to ask you a question, he said. *Are you ready to receive your work? Are you ready for teachings that will appear in the form of a book?*

I said yes, I was absolutely ready. As I did that, the yogi faded out of view, and in his place, Jesus appeared.

He reached out a hand to me and said, *Then start writing.*

Chapter 8

The Call from Jesus

There is so much to be said at this time. We have come up and are coming up so close to a time where the self eludes the self. Meaning, there is a deep unknown territory within that continues to elude the mind, and that is the heart.

The heart is the pathway within. It has always been. The heart is the known place deep inside where you know and feel the Truth is heralded, like knights and kings around the table. Now is this time for it to elude no more. Now is the time for our hearts to awaken to the deepest Self. This is the heart of the Soul. This is the place so deep inside you that there are no true words to capture its deepest expression. Herein lies the challenge.

How does one come up close to those parts that one has been eternally running from? How does one continue to question, to beg, to ask for forgiveness and chase the Love that enraptures? A Love that enraptures the body, the mind and the Soul. How do you seek enrapture? What does it mean? What does it look like? What does it feel like? What does it taste like? How does it leave its mark on you at the end of the day? How does it puppeteer you to a new tomorrow? How does it tempt you and caress you at the same time? How do we truly know what enrapture means?

I know. And I am here to tell you and to deliver to you its fullest expression that I know best. That is to say, my deepest experience of it, as I deliver it to you.

In this day, on this day. In this fashion, on this fashion.

Allow the ancient and modern technologies to merge together to weave a path for this transmission, for this sharing to be fully expressed. Allowing the fruits of *our* labor to be shared with you, the reader, the receiver, the learnèd and the learned.

Allow your mind to open, to be freed of yesterday's teachings and to open up to receive these new transmissions, these new manuscripts of the Divine, for the Divine and from the Divine. As it is *all* Divine. Divine timing, Divine work, Divine sharing and Divine sacrifice. Allow all of this work we are sharing to infuse your heart and Soul.

This is a *true* call, and we are the messengers. Allow the hand that is writing this to be a hand guided by these Divine messages. Allow your Self to not be skeptical of this modality, shall I call it, for it is the oldest modality known to man: to scribe.

Allow this scribe to be that. A scribe. A scribe of the Divine messages brought forth during this time on the planet. This time in consciousness and this time in your hearts. The fervor is real; the fever is high. High in its desire to know more, to receive more and to collect more. Now is the time for the king and queen in you to rise and to stand strong in your heart's convictions and your heart's knowings, for there is Truth in this, I promise you.

Open your heart, breathe into your heart and receive. It is much more difficult than you think. Breathe into the heart to open the heart. It is the only way. And then, keep breathing. When the mind is too active, breathe into the heart. Breathe in white Light. Breathe in Grace. Breathe in Love and breathe in your Self, for you are Love. Allow your Self to receive you in all one piece. All in one piece of naked Soul truth.

Do not turn the other cheek and admonish what I share, for that will be the tendency of your mind, but not your Soul as your Soul knows better. Your Soul knows the Truth of the unknown and the known. Honor the breath that you breathe in with and honor the breath that you breathe out with. For this is Life, this is Light and this is breath (Spirit).

Allow your senses to awaken to a deeper knowing that lies within. Allow your senses to also quiet so that you can sense the stirrings of the Soul. Allow your eyes to be revealed the Truth in what they do not see. Allow your eyes to align with that which your Soul knows. Allow your breath to guide you and show you where you must breathe in and allow in, and where you must breathe out and let go.

Use your breath as a flashlight in the spiritual darkness. When upon those moments where you feel cold inside, isolated, afraid and alone. Use the breath. Breathe in with intention and breathe out with intention. The breath will be the unwavering force that awakens and guides you. Allow it to flow inside you in a whole new way. Breathe in Light and exhale darkness, letting everything unwind.

Allow your Self the magic and beauty of the new beginning, the new blank canvas, the new temple of the Soul and the new church of the mind. Allow an ever-pervasive freedom to wash over you. Allow my Spirit you feel inside your hearts to awaken and resurrect.

Allow your Self to move, and invite the collective to move from Crucifixion to Resurrection. Allow the shift to happen within. To know that we are moving toward a Heaven on Earth. This is the time *now*. The time has come *now*. The *now* is the Resurrection. The Resurrection is in our hearts. Take the time, be the time, make the time. For tomorrow is coming all too soon.

Set your course today to make that change inside. To un-wash the washing of your mind and the collective mind. To breathe in a new day beyond one of any recognition, for the frequency of yesterday is outdated and becoming obsolete. Those of you who stay will get stuck, and those who prevail in their hearts will prevail. Show your Self. Reveal thy Self to your own heart. Reveal your Self to me as I dwell inside your heart. If you do not trust your Self then trust me to receive you. I will embrace you, take your tender heart, hold your delicate heart and wash away your tears.

Hold fast for I am here to embrace you in my hand and in my heart. Outreach your hand and take mine. I will guide you, I will support you and I will reveal to you the Truth that is waiting to be set free. The time has come. You may continue to wander but all you will find is a feeling of loneliness and eventually hate.

What kind of a life is this? You have seen in history the demise of such choices of such wanderers of the heart. Do not allow your Self or your Soul to waste time in this effort for it will pain you, deplete you and distract you from your Soul's Truth. Fear not the barriers in your mind. Give them to me. Fear not the woes in your heart. Give them to me. Fear not the fears of your neighbor. Give them to me. For I am an alchemist of the Light. Give anything to me such as water and I shall stir it into wine. For this is and has been my purpose and my choosing. Give to me and I shall give to you.

Fear not your mistakes, for they too will guide you. They will light the path and show you how much you have to give, to create and to Love. Hold your hands tightly together with mine and we shall walk anew. We shall forge a new path and will ignite your heart and your Soul in ways you have never felt before. Give your Self over—to *Love*. Embrace and embark on this challenge and you shall never be disappointed.

This is my promise to you, from my promise-land to the promise-land in your hearts. Make the change. Be the change. Invite the change. Allow the change. Make a promise in your heart for a new and better tomorrow for everyone and you will see a shift. You will awaken with a new tune in your heart. Let it resound with joy to the world at large and I will continue to guide and to lead you strong.

Forever Be. Forever in Me. As I am in you, through and through. May your day be blessed from far and wide. May your heart be opened from corner to corner and may you sit long enough to hear the whispers in your Soul and find a way to honor them.

I bid you farewell for now.

In Love, Light and Service,

J

Divine Downloads

Download One

As I come here before you to share about the resurrection in your hearts, I also share the story about the lost Compassion in your Souls. This has been an atrocity of sorts across time, through time and in time. This has been the demise of humankind. For without Compassion, the Soul is bare. For without Compassion, the Soul is naked. For without Compassion, the Soul is scared. Allow your Self to be invited to a deeper place that dwells inside your Soul's heart. This is the place where true alchemy reigns from above. This is the place where your true existence shall stand its test. This is the place far deeper than anyone has ventured to go before. And this time is now.

Accept this challenge, if you will, for now is the time for this test to be taken. You have all been prancing for oh so many centuries and lifetimes, but *this* time in your humanity, in our humanity, is where the litmus test is taken, or even considered. For if not, then humanity *will* fail.

Look around you, look above you and look below you. There is such a deep pain, a deep scar within the heart of humanity. This deep pain and deep scar has left another even deeper scar that requires a massive healing in the hearts and minds of humankind. For those who "sit" in their treetops, sheltered from *this* life: You have failed. Yes, this is a strong word, but I ask you to consider where and when you get your hands dirty in the "muck of life?" Where do you and how do you sit on a seat that is dirty? Do you welcome it or do you sit back and find your comfort in the discomfort?

Download Two

Today it behooves us to bring you these messages, this "scribing", this *word. We* sit here on the proverbial "other side," but what if there really *is* no "other side?" What if the "other" is just an illusion? What if the "side" is also an illusion? Imagine there is a land not far away, that *is* like a fairy tale. Imagine all the people, ringing the bells for themselves and others. Imagine all the people ringing the bells of their hearts for themselves, then others. I imagine all the people who *could* ring the bell for others after ringing it for themselves.

The bell we speak of is the bell of Love. That resounding tone in your heart that, when struck in just the right way, rings on high. That time, when allowed to melt with the Light that dwells inside your hearts, creates the most extraordinary sound you have ever felt, seen or heard. Allow your heart to open to more. Allow you heart to open to the bell that rings inside the deepest place that dwells within the corner of your heart.

Allow the breath that you breathe to massage the heart and to bring the Light with each intentional breath. Allow your Self to be seen. Allow your Self to be seen by your Self. Allow your Soul to guide you and to know you. Allow your Self to know it. Allow your Self to be free of what others have left inside your head. Allow your Self to rid the mind of its hallucinations. The ones of manipulation, the ones of greed, the ones of creed and the ones of color. Allow the mind to be freed from everything that weighs it down.

Allow your heart to prevail for it will guide you deeper in the uncharted territory within your Soul's heart. Allow your breath to show you and to guide you in. Allow your Self to take breath upon a new day. Allow your heart to shine and to be shown more today than yesterday. Allow all and all will allow. Trust all and all will give. All will prevail and all will provide. Allow the rhythm of Life to show you and guide you. Allow the flow and trust the flow. There is a flow, there is a current to Life, your Life and all of Life. Allow this current to carry you.

Resistance is futile. Allow the flow to guide you for there is an intelligence in this flow. Allow the flow to flow and then follow it, for it will take to a place where a deeper part of your Soul resides. A deeper place within the heart. Some may call it the "heart math." We call it the Soul's Heart. We call it the place of Truth. We call it the place, the feeling, the domain of where *all* Truth resides.

Your Spiritual Truth, your Soul's Truth and your Heart's Truth. A trinity, if you will. Allow us in this message to guide you and to point even more strongly now to your eternal true north. Allow, allow and allow. We cannot say this enough. Even in true allowing there is a letting go. For if you force into allowing then you create more resistance. It is not a force or a pressure but an intelligence and a feeling. Allow the feeling to guide you and show you.

Allow us here, on the other side, as you perceive it, to undo the binds that tie. Allow us to unfold the folding, neat corners and all. Allow us to show and invite you to explore how and when it can serve and does serve to let go, to mess things up, to let your hair go shaggy and to unfold the neatly folded corners, for in this too, there is Life. For in this too, there is breath. For in this too, there is more. More to be revealed and more to be shared. More to be uplifted and more to uplift humanity. More to bring the Light in, in greater waves, and more to plug into in a deep way.

Allow this frequency that you are receiving through the words on these pages to caress your Soul. Know that this is a book of Life. Know that this is a book that breathes a deeper life. Allow the transmission to ignite you. Just breathe it in off these pages piece by piece. Allow the layers to build and allow some time in-between to integrate.

Allow your Soul to rest in the early evening and integrate these sharings, then drink some more. Drink from the golden cup; the chalice, if you will. Drink into your heart and then drink some more. Allow your Self to be imbued by this frequency of Golden White Light. Allow this book to rest next to you at night, allowing its Life to breathe you, to serve you, to imbue you. Allow your Self now, to rest.

Download Three

As for now is this time, and this is the time that we all must coalesce as one. Coalesce in our hearts *and* in our minds. Meaning to see and to feel in your mind how we can all be One and how we all are One. To come inside the mind of another and to sit down and have some tea. To break bread with each other in your minds as well as in your hearts and Souls. To allow this pure essence, this pure nourishment to pour forth across the table, from one cup into another. To giveth and to receiveth.

To allow your Self to encompass all that you can embrace. For there is healing and there is Love in the holding. There is Love in all that you do, for everything is One and One is Love. It, at times, may not look like or feel like it, but it does and it is. So I invite you to drink and to drink some more from the overflowing cup, the chalice of Pure, Gold, White Light. This is Divine Love, this is pure consciousness.

This is the way. This is the only way. Relax and receive and all can and will come. Relax and receive and you will allow more to come. You see, it is our own selves that hinder the process, that slow down the cultivation of the seeds of consciousness. It is us who forget to water the seeds, who move the proverbial pot into the sun and allow the soil to dry out.

To daily nourish is of utmost importance to connecting to this Higher Love. To daily practice meditation, prayer, gratitude, sharing and caring all bestow such huge gifts that come from on high. The stuff of life is just that. Stuff. At times a distraction, at best a detractor. It takes us away from the highest realm, from the highest form of Love.

To know Oneness, to receive Oneness and to allow Oneness. This is the crutch that lies next to us. How do you find that Oneness from the outside if you need a crutch to walk you inside? What distractions or crutches can you let just fall away? What crutches can you do without? What sidebars will have you removed from your highest calling?

To know consciousness in its purest form, to receive consciousness in the form of Love. To inhabit and inhibit ourselves away from what removes us. Perhaps is it the Self that eludes the Self. Perhaps it is the broken, tender heart that tears through our every pulse. Perhaps it is you and perhaps it is I. Perhaps there is a better way, a higher way. Consciousness is shifting as we are all beginning to feel ourselves and how we connect to the unified field. *That* is the ever changing hologram of the Universe. Each day we wake and feel anew. A part of that anew you are feeling is the shift in consciousness. As it rapidly changes and is changing for the better.

As the boat of Enlightenment is expanding, so too are the oars that row it. Meaning the minds of humanity. The minds of man, woman, child, brother, sister, cat, dog and so on. They are as we are the oars that row the boat of Enlightenment to the shores of Divine Love and Grace. With little effort and a lot of Ease, all things are possible. The Infinite Field of Possibilities is open. It is open to all who want to walk anew. Allow your Self to walk anew. Allow your Self to invite in the Beings of Ease and Grace. Allow them to kick at your door and gently enter. For they know the way.

Download Four

Now there is more to be shared through this hand. This hand is the one who scribes the most clearly. There will be others who say they do as well, but there is a lot of distortion. Meaning there is a lot of big ego. We invite you to feel the Truth of this message in your heart and in your bones.

We invite you to dive more deeply into you—into Self. For it is the Self that holds the key to revelation and salvation. It is you who holds the key. Not I. You are the makers of your destiny. Your own personal destiny and the destiny of humanity. Set time aside to dive more deeply into you and what you will uncover and discover is oh so great, your heart will weep and your Soul will soar.

Allow your thoughts to be cleared. To be moved to the side. To be massaged to sleep. Through the ancient modalities of prayer and meditation, there will be found a healing for the Soul. There will be found your true voice—the voice of a Higher Power that lives inside you. Allow the frequencies of Ease and Grace to support you, to show you and to guide you. For they know the clear oath, the true way, without the ego. The ego is necessary to keep your Self alive, and to do certain jobs, but this is mostly it. Allow your ego to sleep for a while and breathe into your heart as you receive these higher vibrations. These words. This download. These messages. This is the Truth that your heart is looking for.

This is the Truth that will set you free from your illusion that you are not already free. This is the instruction manual, if you will, for the return to the already liberated self. This is the message that will set so many free from their fears about religion, about spirituality and about freedom. Yes, so many of you are afraid of freedom. This is one of the binds that tie as you bind our free selves with the fear of what you are binding. It is a competing intention as some would call it. It is a split Soul, one might say. It is a deeper knife to a wound that is already healing so many other fears. For people are waking up as you call it. People are remembering.

It is *my* duty to be the Light that shines for you. To guide you and to show you the way, when you are lost. For, yes, you are *all* a part of my flock. You are *all* my children. I do not judge, as you might do. For we are a part of me as we are One. All of us are One. Don't you see? We are all connected. We are connected at birth through this Divine Light some might call source energy, God, Truth, Peace, Love, Light, and so on. Fear *not* your fears for they only keep you there, don't you see?

Stay in Love. Stand in Love and all will be well. This is how to create Heaven on Earth. This is the way. This is the path. This is the swell. The tide is turning. Give yourself permission to see the Truth, to feel the Truth and to know the Truth. So help me to help God, if you will. Help me to help the Light. Help me to help the Truth, by allowing your Self to receive.

Test not the waters of the hate and the will for they are strong and turbulent. Test not the waters of the heart for they are choppy like the sea. Test not the waters of the mind for they are succinct in their effort to dissuade. Test only the waters of the Soul, for they are steadfast and strong, like a current that knows where to go. Like a storm that knows where to land. Like a sea that knows how to swell and like a boat that knows how to adjust its sails. Allow your Self to weather more deeply today than yesterday.

Allow your Self; the yin and yang of your Self to breathe together, in unison, in song. Allow the two hearts that live inside you to beat as one. The heart of your mind and the heart of your Soul. The yearnings of the mind can be a distraction of sorts. Allow them to soften and relax under your will. Under the will of God, Under the will of the Light. The God I speak of is not the God as so many of you have learned to be a man on a chair in the sky. I am speaking of God as the father of All. God as the father of humanity. And God as the teacher of All. And with *that* God lives the yin and yang. The feminine and the masculine, as you know it.

The truth is that *it* is all the same, but these deeper teachings take time to digest. So for now, allow me in. Allow you in. For we are One. Allow your Self to be seen. Allow your Self to be seen for who you truly are. Allow your Self to be honed and sharpened to your finest point and then to serve your Self to *all* of humanity. This is the way. This is the New Way. You must go within first, then go out.

Allow your Self to find your truest heart's song and then sing it as loud as you can. Allow your best note to be heard across the land. Allow the ears that will hear you to be Graced with such beauty and sweetness their Souls will cry. Allow any and all glass ceilings to be not only shattered, but to be memorialized by creating the most lovely mosaic man has ever encountered. Allow these mosaics to paint your personal story. Allow these mosaics to serve as a reminder of what wondrous alchemists you *all* are. For each and every man, woman, child and being on this planet has *had to* endure some kind of suffering because this is the time that was and is still being lived.

But I tell you, this is changing. The seas are beginning to swell. The tide is rising to lift all boats. Consider this a spiritual swell. Consider this the greatest swell inside your heart that you have ever known, felt, seen or tasted. For this is the *Truth* that humanity has been waiting for. This is the *Truth* that has allowed you to endure so much. It has been waiting in the wings of life. Sidestage, if you will. But no more shall it be kept silent, for *it* knows, now is the time. There is a deeper intelligence inside *all* of you that knows the tide has risen.

This tide is red. Not for the reason that you might think, but for what it represents to me. This red represents my blood. This is the blood that I wept from my body, from my hands. I wept with blood so that you would take notice. I wept with blood from my hands so that people would notice. So that my story would not go untold. I chose to stay alive on the cross for days and weep. I chose to bleed my story. My story of redemption, my story of Love and Compassion. These are my teachings. This is my legacy.

To tell the Truth of my redemption within my Soul. To allow, finally, for my voice to be heard and to be shared in a clear way, through this clear channel. I find and know this time has come for the Truth to be revealed. For my Truth to be revealed. For *this*, my story, is the salvation of humankind.

Not at the doors to the Kingdom of Heaven in the sky. For the Kingdom of Heaven is awakening in *all* of us. The Kingdom of Heaven lies inside us. Inside you. Inside me. Inside everyone. We are remembering. We are removing the barriers. We are healing. We are praying. We are committed to raising the bar of the Spiritual heart that lies within each and every one of us. We are committed to raising the awareness of all of the unnecessary suffering of humanity. We are here now in this time, to bring the Truth closer to our hearts, as One.

My hands bled. Yes, they did. My feet bled, yes, they did. My head bled, yes, it did. But not as much as my heart was bleeding on the inside. For I wept for years after that day. For I knew the suffering and *that* is what I carried with me. The suffering of humankind, not the shadow of humankind, as some "prophets" would have you believe. **I carried the suffering of the human shadow having to hide.** I carried the pain in everyone's hearts from living in an eternal state of imprisonment.

The shadow not being able to breathe is what has destroyed humanity thus far. It is the denying of the shadow self that has hindered our growth and evolution. It is the yin to the yang. They are both equal in measure. They are both necessary to walk through this thing called life. To successfully walk through suffering and to come out the other side. This is why I wept. To get noticed. To be noticed for days. To allow people to sit or kneel before me and allow the Compassion and

Love in their hearts to rise. *That* is why. I chose this work, with my God. It was of my choosing.

If anyone knew me, as my disciples did, they knew I had a shadow, but I was heralded for my Life and message. My shadow was swept under the rug. I confess, here today, that I was not as kind as I could have always been. I was rude, short-tempered and angry at times. Some things were not depicted in your books, your Bible, as they were my shadow. And the powers that be who wrote the Bible wouldn't have it any other way. I ask you. Who wrote the Scriptures? It says, my men did. But they were long departed when it came time to scribe our time and the teachings from those times.

Who, I ask you, wrote the Scriptures? Men did. A team of men who came together, in the form of a union of sorts. *They decided* what to write. *They decided* what to add and mix in to the passed-along teachings. *They decided* to add some fear. *They decided* to add some manipulation. *They decided* to write things to control the minds and the hearts of Jerusalem. *They decided* to use these heart teachings as a platform to control the masses. *They decided, as men*, to dabble in false claims and false teachings. *They decided* to water down the Love and Compassion of the teachings. *They decided*, as men, to abuse their power as the Patriarchs in that time. *They decided. And they did.*

This atrocity that they committed, for it was, shaped an enormous amount of humankind.

Download Five

Dear Beloved Ones: today the tide has shifted. In my realm and in your realm. The tide has risen. The Light is on. It is all aglow—I wish you could see it. The tide has come and it not only is turning the sorrows of yesterday into the Truth today, but it is here now to show us and to teach us how. The how of the knowing. The how of the Truth and the how of the present. Allow your minds to become more flexible in this here and now. For there are an infinite number of here and nows to come and they will be grander than the ones before them.

For as you stand in your presence and stand in your heart in this here and now, the future here and now will be taken in a deeper stand. Meaning you will be digging in, into a deeper place inside your Self. This is the moment now. This time has come. So we ask you leave your monkey mind to the side. For all it wants to do is to shout and kick and scream and distract you from your hearts' knowing and your Soul Truth. In essence it is a remarkable game. How do we "beat" this monkey at his/her own game? How do you stop the antics of that mind? You just do. And how you do that is by breathing. This is a life long technique that has been taken for granted and that has been deeply misunderstood.

The breath is here as a teacher. To show you and to guide you. *This* is the flashlight in the darkness. *This* is the way home, to your heart and to your glory. *This* breath will guide you, correct you, and show you. Fear not the deeper breath, for he/she knows where to go and what to reveal to you. You must *trust* your breath to show you and to guide you. You must learn to focus on the breath, to relearn the breath. And this breath, will turn *your* tide. For the breath is connected to Spirit. Spiritus. To breathe, to allow, to engulf Spirit. This is the awakening. This is the remembering. This is the Truth that your Soul needs. This is the Truth that your Soul is seeking. Use the breath as *that* flashlight and *All* will be found.

Allow Life to sneak in a little bit more and show you what *is* and what *isn't*. Some might call this a splitting of hairs but it will make sense soon as you dive deeper and delve to understand what is churning inside you. When you find out what is behind that breastbone of yours that so well covers up that heartbeat. The heartbeat of the Divine. Tell not the fear in your heart that all will be fine and well. Drive that fear out with self-love and self-compassion. This is the path to true freedom and liberation. Out that damn spot and it shall never return. Allow poetic justice to speak to you. Allow it in to you. Allow it to find its home in the balance in your heart. Let not the mind distract you as it is now. Breathe. And continue to breathe. Allow, allow and allow. We cannot say this enough.

The "we" is the co-creator and I. The channel, the author, the scribe. Call her what you wish. Call her a witch for she does not care. She has been thrown under the proverbial bus over and over and has received very specific training for this mission. Her Soul is serving. Her Soul is living the Life it intended—as she wished and chose. You may argue her channelings, her downloads, her messages. Call them what you wish for it does not matter. These messages are coded with a frequency that will ignite you at a core level if you allow them in. It is not her job to birth your Spirit, even though she can, as she has that gift.

It is *now* yours. Your job, your time. *This* is the tide that I am speaking of. This is the tide that is now rising. As you all stand more in your Self responsibility. Empowered. In charge. In charge of your Self and more importantly of your Soul. For Life is changing. There is no more time to wait. The time has come. The time is now. The healing has been done—at least enough. This is calling for a higher upgrade. These words will heal as you allow them in and digest them. These words will speak to your Soul in a whole new way. These words will one day become our words as we all soar higher to a Divine realm for new beginnings. New beginnings here on Earth. Let not there be more time wasted. For you are here. You are now.

The spiritual teachers of this time have prepared you well, so now is the time to leave some of that behind as you upgrade to the next level. The higher level of deep Self Love and even deeper Self Compassion. This upgrade will not take long, for there is not enough time to wait. The planet and humanity cannot endure anymore suffering. This has to stop and it is stopping. *Now! With You!*

Imagine humanity loving itself? There would be no war. There would be no famine for there would be no need for fear or control. These dogmas are all lies. They hold no Truth. They are just an illusion. An Illusion of the heart. Your Soul knows this Truth. The Soul always recognizes a lie. We have all just been coached to not listen to the Soul. To pay credence to the mind and all its keepings. To the monkey mind, the outlandish mind, the fear-based survivor mind, the rookie mind, the mind's mind. There is an ultimate program that runs the mind and this is the lie. This is the illusion. *Let not* these times go to waste. *Let not* this time now be wasted again. For it will try to be and part of it—it will want you to. That is—the mind. That is what it does. So as you begin to recognize it more and more—what it wants from you, how it distracts you, how it deludes you—take no notice. Accept if your mind is taking you more in to where you truly want to go. Where your heart and Soul want to go. Let go of the ego-desire with the hard edges. Instead tap into what the ego desires from a fun and playful place. Like a new car. It can reside in both places. Check your intention and from where you are connecting. Both are ego, one is just much lighter and less frivolous than the other. There is nothing wrong with the ego, as long as it knows it is the ego.

Allow the binds that tie in the mind to be loosened. Be aware when they are holding tight or feel tight. Be aware of the programmed mind and what it wants to tell you. Be aware of the programming and wants you do not listen to, such as these messages. Be aware that you have been given the gift and the freedom of excellent free choice and free will. You choose. Your mind does not. Your Soul gets to choose. The mind does not. The will gets to choose. The mind does not. Know that you, as your Soul, are the eternal driver in the seat and not the passenger. Know that you hold the keys, not the machine of the mind that just wants to grind away and be done with Life a way. The mind gets tired. The mind will convince you that you are tired when you are not. It is a very different sensation from what you are used to feeling. Take it for a test drive and see. You will soon discover to what we are referring. There is alchemy in all. Trust in that. Let Life flow to you and watch the magic alchemize. Fear not change, for change brings growth and growth brings a spring, a spring to the Soul.

Let not the matters of the mind interfere with the matters of the heart. Allow the mind to take a quiet rest and ignore its own musings. Allow the nest inside your heart to receive those things, those heeds for new beginnings. For new pathways, for new mindways.

Download Six

Today, there are musings to talk about. Musings of the mind and musings of the heart. Today, we will stand more deeply in our hearts. Today, we will take a stand for Love. Today, we will take a deeper stand for Compassion. Today, you will blend the two together and take your Soul to new heights. Today, you will understand more completely than ever before, why now is *the* time for this. As we have said there is a musing and there is a turning. This turning is the turning of a tide within. This turning is a turning of the tide wishing your heart to deliver not from evil, as this is somewhat of an illusion. But to turn away from what has transpired in the past. To turn away from some of the teachings that have been shared and spread. For *all* of these teachings were not just *that*. Meaning they were not just teachings, but they were manipulations. Manipulations of the mind and manipulations of the heart. This was done with intention. This was done deliberately. Know that all of that was done across time, through time and in time, with a *very* deliberate focus to bind humanity and create the illusion that you are not already free. To understand what is being expressed here takes great patience, a great open mind and an even greater open heart. So, to understand these newer teachings is going to require an even deeper opening in the Soul. For even the Soul has been programmed with these false teachings and manipulations.

Even the mind cannot understand what has transpired in the last thousand years. It is an understanding that must come from the Soul. The "clean Soul." For the Soul too can be manipulated. Yes, it is an atrocity, have no doubt. Yes, a crime has been committed, have no doubt. This is *not* about a conspiracy. This is about a healing. This is about a deeper understanding of who you are and who you are not. You are not your programs of belief systems. You are more than that. You are not the beautiful and injured Soul. You are more than that. You are the stars in the sky that have fallen to Earth. You are the stardust that makes up your skin, hair and bones. You are pure magic. You are pure Light. You are pure Grace.

Enjoy these musings from my heart to yours. Enjoy the words as they simply appear on your paper. Enjoy these heraldings as they wash and caress your Soul. Enjoy this energetic poetry as it moves over your heart and touches it with its gentle hand. Enjoy these times and this time for it opens a doorway and a pathway within to a deeper place, a deeper yonder, a deeper knowing, a deeper Truth. Enjoy this time here in the now. In this right now. Again, in this right now. Now breathe. Feel the energy shift? That is *it*. That is where we are going, that is where we standing. In the new. In the new mind, in the new heart and in the new Soul. This is a huge purging, detoxing and dumping of bad data one might say. This is the new way of being.

This is the second coming. The second coming is *me*, is *my* word, with out the heresy and with *deeper* Truth. This will be heard for it is time and those of you that know this is the time, *know* it is the time. For those of you who understand that humanity is asking for and calling for a *deeper truth*. For those of you that know, *this* time is *now*. The time *is* now. Understanding the time the world is in and understanding the time we are in in humanity and in consciousness is of the utmost importance. Allowing the *real truth* to be spoken, to be read and to fly free.

These teachings are not and will not be for everyone as there are different waves of consciousness that we swim in. There are many fish in the sea to fish. But this idea and this offering is a new golden gilded fish. A new fish. One that has not been offered before. We understand there will be fear. Fear of the potential shakedown. Fear of the unknown. Fear of the scars that will be revealed. Fear of even being free, as this can feel overwhelmingly uncomfortable. This will bring in a new way of being, a new way of thinking and a new way of being. As other spiritual teachers offer the idea of *beingness*. Ask your Self perhaps what this actually might mean to you on a deep personal level. I invite you to contemplate it. Allow your mind to *open*. Allow your heart to fly free. Allow your ideas and your non-ideas to be born. Allow your Soul to talk. Allow your Soul to chat to you and with you. Allow your Self the quiet time *it* takes, *it* requires to inhabit this new space and place inside your Soul. For it is an infinite well of possibility. It exists in the infinite field if we let it. It exists in the infinite field of your heart if you let it. It exists in the infinite well of the Universe. It rocks back and forth to emulate a smooth slumber. To evoke from the mind a smooth idea of transition back into the Soul. For to see what the Soul is, to feel what the Soul feels, takes a lifetime or many of practice.

These are the musings from my heart to yours. These are the knobs and switches that will turn you *on*, to a higher calling. A higher wavelength. A higher vibration of Being. Rest not in your heart. Dive deep into your Soul and poke around. Ask questions. Beseech your gifts that lie in wait. Move not the hands of the clock forwards or backwards, just simply sit, unwind and be still. There is knowing in this practice. There is stillness in this practice.

Allow your Self to be seen for who you really are. Allow your self to be seen for the next level of whom you came here to be. Allow your Self to be seen for all that you *are*. For *all* of your Glory. For *all* of your Light. For all that you offer and all that you bring. Turn off the Light in the mind and search for the Light in your heart. Know that once you find this bright Light in your heart that you are halfway there. Not that there is truly nowhere to go, because you all have already inside you what you need. *Those* knobs and switches are just being turned back on one at a time.

What if when Beelzebub fell to Earth he cursed humanity?

What if when he cursed humanity, the curse was Karma?

Do you see? It is a *forever* loop of suffering. To be measured, to be judged in the everyday understanding of the word Karma, as in "good Karma," "bad Karma."

What if your suffering is an illusion in a whole new way?

What if Karma has become the spiritual straitjacket that has tied up all of humanity?

What if there is a new energetic flow to life? What if there is a new energetic overflow and evergreen? Meaning, what if there was a whole new reality waiting for us?

What if this new reality is Heaven on Earth?

And what if this reality exists right now in this very moment and this reality is sitting right next to you?

Download Seven

What if this time is timed? What if this time, this new wave of consciousness has a limited wave to it? What if there is a certain time frame or time allowance in the cosmos where and when this movement *must* take place. What if the cosmic window is now open but will not be open forever, for this movement to take flight? What if all of *you* are imperative to this shift?

What if you *all* stood in your personal power and your personal truth of the Truth? The real Truth that has been a mystery for most. A real Truth that has been guiding most, but unknown to most. The real Truth that has been woven in and throughout the cosmos and the Universe. The Truth that is the liberating Truth. And that is that *you are God!*

Yes, what if the liberating Truth is that you are all God, dressed in sheep's clothing, meaning you are and have been hiding? What if the Truth is not the idea of God and Love and Light, but that you are God and Love and Light? Not because there is a mystery behind this uncovering, but that there is Truth in the simple Truth that you Are. You Are. You are It. And so you shall Be. This is the Truth that has been eluding so many for so long. This is the Truth that shall set you all free! It is not something outside of you, above you or behind you that you are seeking. It is not even right in front of you. It is *in* you! You are *It*!

So, I invite you to breathe that in. Again, I invite you to breathe that in. Breathe... How does that feel? Strange? Bizarre? Wonderful? Magical? Obscene to some? Perhaps. Perhaps not and that's all right. It's all alright. Do you see all of the judgement that comes up around this offering? That's the spiritual conundrum. The judgment is what binds you. It binds the heart. It binds the mind and it binds the matter that we call Earth. So the question remains with what to do with some of the doubt that you may have around this?

This is the most riveting question. This is the curious beast inside you that wants answers. Curiosity can be playful and fun and it can be a ravenous teacher, guide and guru. Listen to your curious mind. What is it asking of you? It is asking you to be open. It is asking of you to consider a different alternative. Sometimes, the curiosity can act like breadcrumbs to force open an already forced shut mind. A determined mind that is made up. Do you see how this cannot serve the wanderings of your heart? Do you see how this shutness cannot out what needs to be outed?

Allow your heart to feel what it *wants*. Acknowledge your heart and its yearnings. Be not a stranger to your heart for it is you. You and your heart are one. Do not try to salvage pieces of a heart that has gone astray. Trust the strayness of your heart as it holds a vast intelligence that you cannot even begin to comprehend. Trust it as it guides you to push forward, to do better, to listen to itself, to cultivate more awareness, to cultivate more Self Compassion, and to cultivate more Self Love.

Allow that keeper of your heart, that is you, to listen closely as you navigate the waters and adjust your sails. Trust the sails once you have set a course from this place, to take you to where you are pointing. Trust the flow. Trust the process. Trust Life.

Trust is something that waxes and wanes in all of your hearts. Mine once did too. I had fear. I had doubt. Then I committed to the untold Truth of my day. That Faith was a choice, not a way of being. That Faith was the thing to honour, not the so-called word of a church. And so I stand here today in front of all of you once again on a cross of sorts. But this time it is different. For I am stronger. I am knowing as I am free.

There will be no crucifixion for that is an old tale. It was important for a while, but today it is not. Today is about moving forward. Today is about moving beyond.

Today is about being free. Today is about bloodshed. Meaning, the blood that I shed long ago was to be noticed. The time I took to bleed was a calling of your hearts, of the hearts of humanity. The time I took to hang was a calling to the deeper place inside of most, that I knew was *going* to die and that *was* dying.

This was the way that I was shown where humanity was going. So I became a messenger of a great message. The message of Love and Compassion. The message of the new way that has taken many years to come. And not in vain, I might add, for this time is of the most important time.

This time is the Resurrection. This time is the Second Coming of Love and Compassion. It has taken all of these years for humanity to arrive at a cross roads within its collective heart. A crossroads that has created such strife for so many. As one can witness in the temperature of many countries' political climates. There is so much Yin and Yang. There is so much Love and Hate. There is so much black *or* white. And there is not much place for the many shades of grey. Yet…

Download Eight

This time of which I speak, this time that I bring to you asks that you open your mind to the many shades of grey. These shades of grey are a representation of the pains that lie within. They allow all that is being held in pain inside to shine. Yes…to shine. Not a word ordinarily chosen to describe such things, such pains. But they do shine. Because you shine. Allow all of the sparkly-ness to shine. To show and to illuminate. For when the pains are brought out of the shadows, they are immediately brought into the Light. In the Light there is healing. In the Light, there is Oneness. Where there is Oneness, there is Unity. Where there is Unity, there one stands in the totality of Love.

To stand here, to find your place here in the seat of Love, on this planet called Earth. To allow the tide to raise, to rise within the heart, washing your heart. To breathe…to allow the breath to show you, to guide you, to be the wind in your sails, to be the intelligence in your heart. Set sail in your mind and you will know the Truth that lives, breathes and resides inside you. It will know you and you will know it. Allow my breath, the breath of God to illumine you. Move your focus to the breath. Allow it to breathe you. Allow it to flow inside you, around you, within you and without you. Allow, allow, allow.

Stand tall. Stand proud. Be tall. Be proud. Proud that you have chosen to stand tall in these keepings. That you have chosen to stand tall in these offerings. In these waterings in the garden of your Soul. Follow the intelligence in your Soul. For those who do not wish to follow or to even walk, we will pray for them. We will pray together for them to find the Light as they have lost and forgotten their way. They have been pulled off the side of the proverbial road and been offered a cup of distraction. Do not waste time, peeking into this cup along side them.

Keep the focus, keep the Faith, that all will be well and that all is well. Keep me alone inside you, for I am your guide. Trust me to show you and to lead you. Let not your Self be led astray by other false prophets, if they are real and they do exist. Their messages are full of distortion in the end. You will experience a temporary rise from their teachings, but you will find you might only get so far. You might stay looping if you will, in the cycle of Samsara (suffering), because they do not hold the high frequency of Truth. The Light that I offer you from within your Self. I am the gateway to higher consciousness. It is my Divine duty to hold the door open for you, dear Soul. It is my honor and gift to share with you these teachings. It is my duty to serve the highest calling of God. I am filled with Ease and Grace more abundantly each and every day as I pour forth to you from my overflowing and my overflowing cup of Divinity. Be still and listen to your beating heart for it emulates the heartbeats of the Earth, of Pachamama. To let your Soul reside within her. To let your Self cocoon in her. To let your Self be known to her. She is an embodiment of the Divine Mother. She is the one way to your inner Truth, Stillness and Peace. She is the one who Loves you. Let her show you. Take rest in her. Take rest in her bosom of branches and birds. Allow your Self to be seen by her. Allow your Self to be seen through her lens. Allow your Self to be seen as she sees you. As the innocent, playful child, who pitter patters her/his feet on the breastbone of the Mother. It tickles her senses to see you shine. To hear your laughter and to sense your freedom. To feel how you *let* your Spirit soar and sing while playing on her. While her heartbeat is caressing your Soul with every step you take. She invites you, by simply beating, to delve deeper inside your Self and inside your Truth. Stand tall and know that you are being watched, held, loved, supported by this one embodiment of the Divine Mother.

Download Nine

Allow this time to be a time for you to breathe and breathe some more. Allow *all* to flow through you, in you, and around you. Allow this poetry in motion you call Life to adorn you and adore you. Let your heart be the vessel that opens to the stone's throw from the Universe and the Multiverse. Know that there are layers, dimensions, time-stopping interludes, questions, answers, queries, koans, non-answers. Truth, non-Truth. It all exists. It all pervades you. The macrocosm and the microcosm.

The Truth shall set you free is an understatement. You are already free as you are already the walking Truth. You are the walking sun in a land where there are too many shadows. There are so many shadows that are asking, almost begging, to be illuminated. To be illuminated in a way that has not been illuminate before.

To be illuminated with a Light from the breath of fire. This fire is the breath of Life. This breath is the fire of Life. The underpinnings of the mind are the bane of *so* much existence. The falsehoods, the teasings of the mind, the seduction of the mind. The allowance that we allow and give to our mind must stop now. Now, the time has come and it is here. It is within us, around us and it *is* us. Allow these thoughts to flow through. Allow *all* the belief systems and constructs to flow freely from the mind and you shall experience your own freedom on a whole new level. Let not the mind deter you from your fate. You see, this is a choice-point in and of humanity. This is a gift, this choice-point, to let your mind be free and to delve more deeply in your heart. The time has come. The time is now. To trust the ebb and flow of the heart. To trust the insatiable yearnings from and in the heart. To allow the body and the Soul to take you and to show you. To allow it to lead you in such a way you almost walk hypnotically. *Trust* the yearnings within the Soul, for it is the only way. It is the only way home to the door of your heart you see.

We are in time, this time of consciousness where the Soul and the heart are reuniting as one. That is true Oneness. A Oneness within the Self, for the Self. The gift of Self to Self. Allow your heart to speak to your Soul. Invite your Soul to listen to your heart. For they are not mere bedfellows, but they are like the Ginger Rogers and Fred Astaire of a higher consciousness that awaits a new day like the breath from the fresh morning dew that pervades the Spiritual ethers with her great mystery and knowing.

Trust in me, that I will show you and guide you. Trust in my Light as I show you the how and the how not. Trust in the higher consciousness that I bring to you and gift to you. It is yours for the asking and it is yours for the taking. Just remember to choose to ask. Remember to choose to take. For as you are imparted on this human journey called Life, you have been given the extraordinary gift of free choice and free will. And it *is* a gift. Please use it as such. Weigh every choice you make—consciously. Weigh it with your heart, not just with energies. Take the time to consider the heart of the other as you choose this way or that way. Consider their feelings. Consider their heart. Consider their Soul. Consider that this, this choice, that they have chosen, may actually not be for their highest and best interest. Consider that what their body or their personality or ego might want, might not be in their highest Truth.

So as you come together within your Self as One, in Oneness with your own breath, consider that what you might be gifting to another might not be in their highest soul's interest. Please, take the time, heed the time and do not rush in. Tread slowly, tread lightly, tread softly. Some Souls are just more gentle than others, but they do not know it yet. So, if you feel and know this of someone, take the time, slow things down, serve in softness and all will be well.

Download Ten

Allow your Self to breathe and all will be well. Allow your Self to be heard. Allow your Self to sing. Allow your Self to sing on High. Allow your Self to be seen. Allow the world to see you for who you are in all its glory. Allow your Self to be shown the true expression of your Soul, of your calling, of your path and of the Divine that lives and breathes within you. Allow all of your notes to be heard. To be shared. To be revealed. To be uncovered. To be shared. To be shared with All. Then All will know the greatest gift that has been lying in wait in the wings of Life. 'Tis such a magnanimous gift. To allow the Soul to fly free in the face of fear. To allow the Soul to fly open in the face of fear. To allow the Soul to heed the warning and to go ahead anyway. To birth a new humanity from its suffering. To free all Souls from the karmic return. To allow the Souls that require a rewiring, if you will, to allow *them* to be freed from the loop of karmic suffering.

Allow this teaching to stir the Soul inside you. To awaken the sleeping Souls across time and space. To allow the Bells of Freedom to be rung across the land. To ring the Truth that is to be known and carried without any more cover-up, diversions or distortions. To *know* that in the end, you are all already free. The stories, the drudgery, the weight of the unforgiven, of the lessons unlearned, of the stories untold. To hear on high the Truth that you are *so* close to being free in the heart, in the mind and in the body and in the Soul.

Upon the return of the Soul to its Self, there is a prevailing freedom that effuses the Self. It too is an untold story that needs to be shared, heard and retold over and over again. Now is the time for this idea, this teaching to fly free in the Spiritual wind. For the turbines of the Soul to hear, acknowledge and free its Self from its own suffering. To awaken to a higher level of consciousness. To lean in to the deeper awakening that you are who are you are and you are also more. The more is where the Soul wants to go. The more is where the Soul wants to live and wants to sleep. The more is where the idea lives and reigns that you are already free. What if this is the second coming? What if this is the all-knowing high Truth that everyone is seeking, but nobody knows it by name? What if the suffering is an illusion and the Soul is crucifying itself?

What if the karmic return is the return to freedom? What if the return to freedom is the return that all Souls have been seeking but become stuck in the karmic loop, if you will?

What if the karmic loop *is* the suffering?

What if the karmic looping is a curse placed on Earth as Beelzebub fell from above?

What if the fall is the curse? What they are one and the same?

What if the Garden of Eden still lives and prevails inside everyone's hearts and Souls?

What if the Garden of Eden is alive and well inside each and every one of you?

What if the story you have been told across time, through time and in time is a lie?

What if the ideas that you have been told about my teachings are a lie?

What if these lies have been fabricated by man in order to manipulate and control the masses?

What if the Truth isn't out there, but it has been inside you the whole time?

What if the liberated Self is alive and well inside you?

What if the liberated Self already knows its Self?

What if the liberated Self already knows its Self and is in the process of undressing itself?

What if the undressing is the healing process?

What if the healing process is asking us to light a fire to burn away all of the atrocities, the karmic suffering, the story and burdens we carry around relentlessly, suffering, over and over again? Looping, around and around and around.

What if there is a land out there called Father Earth and that Earth is a twin Earth to this Earth and that Earth embodies a twin of our selves that lives, dwells and breathes Life without any karmic suffering? Completely detached from story or stories?

What if that Earth is the way out or the New World as some teachers say?

What if there is a sight to be seen at such an extraordinary rate, that it tickles the senses and soothes the Soul?

What if it has nothing to do with this Life and everything to do with that Life?

What if we are actually inhabiting the "wrong life?"

What if that is the ultimate gift of free choice and free will?

What if we get to choose which way to go or which door to choose?

What if the door has been open all the time but we just had to choose to walk through it or not?

What if there is a part of us that is afraid to let go of the suffering?

What if there is a part of us that is afraid to let go of *everything?*

What if you let go of everything that is no longer serving you? Yes, *you.*

What about awakening more to your own Divinity? Removing obligation. Removing obstacles to joy and freedom. Removing people or relationships in your life that tether you down.

What if there was a relationship exchange based on no exchange at all? Just pure joy and bliss of spending time together, living together, enjoying each other until the joy stops flowing?

What then?

What does that world or paradigm look like? The world might look a lot freer, a lot less demanding, a lot less stressful. A lot less obligation and a lot less torturing of the Soul.

Download Eleven

Today is another day. A day to ponder upon and a day to wonder upon. To never lose touch or lose sight of that which nurtures you, holds you and guides you. To always allow the effervescence of Life to flow through you, to adore you and to Love you. To not allow the naysayers to say nay. To not allow the deterrers to deter. For if this is your calling and this is your path, then so it is and so it shall be. Wonder and continue to wonder who you are. What you are made of? Why you are here and where you are going?

Continue to allow all of the beautiful questions and ponderings of the mind to percolate to the surface and nourish your Soul. Allow the nectar of this Life to fill you and feed you. For what if you only had one Life? What would you do differently? Would you do anything differently? What would you do the same? Would anything change? Could anything change? What is pre-destined and what is choice? How do we know? How do we discern? How do we unveil the Truth of what we speak, of what we say, of what we see around us and of what we seek?

Allow all of these odd and obscure muses of the mind to unveil. Allow all of the ideas of theming to stir water into wine. For you see, this is how to manifest. This is how to create. To first Imagine. Imagine all the people. Imagine them how, you ask? Imagine a whole humanity free. Free from "sin," free from guilt. Free from shame.

Free from hatred. Free from resentment. Free from life-threatening anger and free from lust that fosters addiction. Imagine that all that you choose in your mind creates your reality. Imagine you have and host a mind so powerful that you could defy natural law. Imagine that pigs had wings. If everyone on the planet imagined that pigs could fly, would they once perhaps grow wings?

Imagine that all of your ideas are storehouses within a library within the Universe and they only can become a reality when someone takes the book out and decides to follow your ideas. They create a movement. For a leader must have a follower to create a movement. The Yin and the Yang to creating change on this planet. The Yin and the Yang to creating a long-awaited change for a better humanity. Meaning a freer humanity. A better, faster, cleaner way to create and manifest more liberation and freedom. A better and clearer way to be free. To be free of the self in a way. To be free of that same mind that can create as it can also punish. The monkey in the mind that exists to derail us, to deter us and to take us off course. The monkey in the mind that has designed and created a circus so grand for itself that it thinks it is running the show. The monkey in the mind that thinks it knows best. The monkey in the mind that will tell you fortunes so grand. It will coerce you and seduce you into thinking they are true when they are not, and in fact, couldn't be further from the truth as they are all illusions. Illusions of the mind. And illusions of the Soul. Even the Soul thinks it is separate from source. The Soul can get stuck. The Soul can be injured. The Soul can fragment and be frozen in time.

What if we could melt the frozen pieces? What if we could sustain a new humanity so grand on the nourishment from our All-Loving hearts? What if we can break this illusion of separateness? What if we can feed our selves and others from that place of Light deep inside the Soul that knows it is whole and complete. What if we can see the delusion of the illusion for what it is? A falsehood. A story. A story so wholly incomplete that it robs the senses of their higher knowing. That feeling that comes over you from time to time that says: There is more than this Life, I am more than this Life. There is something more that exists out there than what we see, feel and hear here. We are more than the here and now. We are more than our senses. We are more of the more. We are truly infinite. You are truly infinite. Allow your Self to breathe in this idea that you are more than what you see, hear and feel. That you see, hear and feel *more* than you understand that you do. Know that you feel and know at time the mystery of The Great Mystery. Know that *that* you feel is *very* true. It is a Higher Truth that resonates at a Soul level. It is the vibration of a Higher Truth that you know and feel. Don't deny this Truth or feeling. Don't allow this feeling to go to waste. Allow this feeling to fill you up and to show you and guide you Home to the Higher Home that lives inside you, around you and through you. Allow *All* to be known, to be known.

What if we could create Heaven inside us with two beings (us and another) and anchor that energy and impregnate the Earth?

Download Twelve

Here we find ourselves. Getting. Pulling. Reaching. Striving. Always encouraging. Often pushing forward. So when do we rest? We rest when the work is done. We play when the work is done. Why? Because time is running out for humanity and planet Earth, or should we say planet Water? Why? Because we are all more Water than Earth. Why? Because that is how Life and God made us.

I come here to you now because now is the time. Now is the time to breathe, the time to move and the time to shake. Shake about what you ask? About whatever deep down is troubling you. What is troubling your body, your mind, your heart and your Soul. What do we do? We shake it off. We shake and dance and dance and shake with great intention to release any and all trauma from the body, at a very deep cellular level.

So I come to you again today to not only stand tall in your heart but to stand tall in your cells. Take me more deeply into you. Breathe me all the way in to a cellular level. Breathe the breath of Spirit into every nook and cranny in your body. Into every crack, into every break, into every place where Light does not shine. This is the work, if you will. All you have to do is breathe and I will be there. All you have to do is trust and I will be there. All you have to do is witness and I will be there. All you have to do is wait and I will be there. All you have to do is know and I will be there. All you have to do is Be and I will Be there. All you have to do is submit to whatever pain and I will be there. All you have to do is know that I will Be there and I will Be there.

Surround your Self and your heart with the deepest knowing that I am always there. Guiding you. Showing you. Surprising you. Trust in my Light. Trust in The Light. We will always be guiding you, showing you, if you let us. Let us show you. Let us guide you. Let us know you and your heart. Allow us in and then breathe. With each breath of breathing us you will breathe in a new way of being. You will breathe in a new way to be deeply personal with your Self and all of what Life and the world has to offer you. What your friends can offer you, what your church can offer you and what your family can offer you. In no particular order, these are *all* fruits of the One Love. Of Divine Love.

Stand tall in your convictions of your heart. Stand tall in your knowing that *all* will be well. Stand tall in your insight that *all* is in the flow. Stand tall. *All is* well.

Let not your mind again deter you from such knowings, such hopes and such dreams. Your dreams have already been set forth in motion. What if your dreams are a pre-cognitive insight into what we, The Light and Life have in store for you? What if dreams are the ideas and events we already know are unfolding? What if pleasant night dreams of your future are just a postcard from your higher self, letting you know that you are on track in this moment?

What if all that you see and know pre-cognitively is *only* a glimpse of *all* of the beauty and wonder that is coming your way. Hold onto this Truth during your times of doubt. Hold onto these images as you make your way through "the muck." Allow these images to be your touchstone. To keep you going while you face the storms of Life. We *all* need this. Everyone needs a touchstone. For some, it is church, family, loved ones, a vision board, a book, a bar, a nightclub. You decide what is the best for you while staying away from the judgment around the choices of others. No body stays in one place forever because Life has bigger plans for them *and* for each and every one of us. Let not the choices of others deter you from your own. Let not your heart and mind be swayed for what you have chosen for you and your highest and best interest. That is not your business; that is "God's business."

Download Thirteen

Today is the day where all things do and all things don't. Let not the deterrents of the mind guide you and sway you. Let your heart be the one to guide you *first* and your mind second. Allow your Soul to shine through. Allow the best and brightest of you to shine on and shine down. Let your heart be true and be true to your heart. Let your sadness be heard and rejoice in your joys. Let your man be loved or your woman be loved. Let your children laugh and let them scream with delight if that is what they need. Let the voices of their Soul be heard. Honor them. Hold them and honor them some more.

Allow your Self to be forgiven for your mistakes. Allow your Self to be heard in your heart too. For you to have feelings for you too are human. If you do not share those feelings then all will be lost. Meaning, the path of the heart will be lost and the journey of the heart will be lost. For you see, we cannot sit and listen and teach others or show others how to feel if we are not feeling our own hearts. *We* cannot persuade others to follow their hearts when we do not follow our own. To listen to our hearts and our own stirrings within our hearts is how we awaken a new humanity. A humanity with more heart and a humanity with more Soul. That, you see, is where our fate lies. Just inside that edge of the beautiful brim of your heart space, your heart chakra, your loving heart, your kind heart, your Christ heart and so on. All of these hearts I mention are all of the hearts of humanity that make it so Divine.

Please be free! Because you already are. So just *be* what you already are. Don't you see? It is right inside of you. The suffering? It is an illusion. You are already free of all that pulls you down. Call up your Free Self. That is where the key lies. In his hand, in her hand. Call upon your wildest imagination of your most Free Self and see what you can come up with. Know and feel in your heart that your most Free Self *is* your most Authentic Self. No lies. No deceit. Just Truth. Just *You*.

Allow today to nurture you. Allow today to nurture all of you. Allow today to breathe new *life* into you. Allow today to fill you up with the air that you breathe, but today do it differently. Do it more consciously. Do it proudly. Do it loudly. Your breath is *life*. Without it there is no gift. So, cherish the breath, cherish the Light that gives you breath. Cherish the sun and the moon and the stars that your human eyes afford you to see. For one, you will not see them as you see them now. Every moment should be savored, as this moment and that moment will never be experienced again. So, rush? What's the point? Where are you trying to go? To find another moment more precious than this one? This moment, right now, you reading this, is a miracle...smile and breathe. It's all here. It's all happening. The joy, the sadness, treat it all as equal and you will learn to honor your human Divinity as the you before you has never done. Do you see? You are the changing miracle all the time. Growing, learning, changing, breathing...

This moment is the first. Never to be repeated again. Similar? Yes, but *never* the same. Savor the moments. Enjoy your friends and family as they show up now, today, not how they were before, for everyone is growing, learning and changing. That is a fact. If they are not, then they are stagnant and most likely feeling physically tired.

Allow your Self to be free of any and all expectation and demand. This is what creates our suffering. To wait for something that might not come. Instead, switch into Gratitude and see how things change around you. She will Love you more. He will Love you more. *If* they don't, perhaps "they" have a hard time with the practice of receiving.

Download Fourteen

Allow your heart and mind to be free. To be free of all these conundrums. All of these musings goad the mind that wants to be free, that wants to find liberation. All of the beautiful ideas and thoughts that want to be free. Allow the tide of time to turn these things over to a higher hand. To my hand. Take my hand and let me show you the way. The middle way of a Truth so deep in your heart that nothing can shake it. A Truth so free in your mind that no one or no negative thought or playful monkey can interrupt the vibration of the idea of Truth. Stay true to your heart's yearnings. Let not the opinion of others sway you. Let not the interruptions of others deter you. Let not the desires and needs of others keep you away from the magical work that God has put you here on this planet at this time to serve with your creative hand. Let not your friends take you away from your dreams.

Always, always, always dream higher than you ever could or can imagine. Sounds silly, but try. The sky is not the limit. There is no limit. Boundaries and limitations of the mind are for fools, for they know not how they choose to repeatedly shoot themselves in the foot, over and over and over, until their pain is so great they find another foot, even yours, to shoot at as well. Stand aside as they endeavor to impale themselves on themselves. For suffering is an illusion and they are only crucifying themselves. Endeavor to be and live the shining example of self Love and Forgiveness. Two virtues that cannot and will not be removed from the Sacred Heart that I am and that you are. That you were born into your natural state. That which you were given by your birthright. That which you were told was not True is an actual fact that stands in Truth.

Compare not your heart to that of a summer's Eve. Compare not your fears to the worst nightmare you have ever known. Allow your heart full of all its fears to be honored, to be held sacred and to be cherished in all its beauty. Allow the Truth that lives and breathes in your heart be heard. Allow the musings of your heart to be shared to bring healing to the land of so many lost in their traumas and addictions. Allow all of the "Hail Marys" to not be in vain. Allow all of your Truth to be seen. Allow your Truth to be heard. Allow your intuition to be heard by your heart. Allow your song to be sung. Allow your best high note to be chanted across the land. Let not the bemusers be heard. Let not the naysayers sing high. Let not the atrocities of the mind interrupt the beautiful flow that falls from your heart.

Let not the disturbances of the past sway you too and fro. Alter your course. Make her sure and steady. Create and craft each day. Allow your voice to be heard each day. Allow your song to be sung each day. Allow the Love and Light to flow from your heart. Breathe in the healing energies that infuse these pages. Make your recovery your highest priority. Make you, your highest priority, Fear not of being selfish, for it can be a self-wish.

Allow the musings of time to amuse you. Allow the hands of time to guide you. For Father Time knows the best seasons for things to bud, for you cannot force a rose to open. Time, rain, sun and the eternal clock of Mother Nature foster our Spirit when we find ourselves impatient. Trust that Life has an agenda for you and the more you push your agenda, the tighter things get. So, breathe, relax and relax some more. Things are all in hand if you have "done your work." Most of you reading this have "done your work." Let not the voice of the negative Spiritual ego convince you that you have not and that there is more work to be done for you to be "worthy." Simply align with the birthright of your worthiness. And all shall feel and be well.

It is the deep-seated feelings of unworthiness that interrupt our flow of abundance in all forms. It is the tide that erodes the shore of our deepest wishes and desires. So we bring the antidote. The antidote of Love, Trust and Skill. The skill of remembrance. Remembering who we are, who we were and where we came from. Remembering the Glory of God that lives and dwells inside us. Remembering our Light. Remembering our spark of Divinity. Remembering *you*.

Remembering *us*. Remembering all of *us*. Calling forth the Divinity in each and every one of us to rise. To rise in remembrance of your true nature. To rise in remembrance of the solitude in your heart that knows it is made of pure gold. To rise up in your heart for Self and for other. To rise up in Love. To rise up in Patience and to rise up in Strength. Finding the quality of a strength inside the heart called Valour. A Valour of an ineffable quality that when struck from the outside strikes back in denial of such a blow. Such a Valour of the heart cannot be broken for it is from Divine Love. One may try to break the Spirit, but the Spirit prevails for it is stronger. It is faster. It is lovelier. It is unbreakable as it comes from the Light and the Light always wins. As my devotion to the unforeseen atrocities on the cross.

My Light never broke for my Soul knew its calling and its purpose. I too have been covered in thorns as you have. I too remember what it was like and I walk with you, hand in hand, holding you steady when you are weak. Holding you up when you feel like falling. And sheltering you from a storm when the rage is too much and you need some respite. When you have been wrongfully accused, I will nourish you when you come to me. But you must come and drink from my cup. We must co-create together a journey of Oneness. We must join forces together to awaken those who are sleeping. For those sleeping are those who do not remember. We want them to remember. Will you help me to awaken them?

Download Fifteen

Let us be true to all our hearts' desires and wants. Let us be true to all that we have been given and that that we have forgiven. Let us be true to the summoning that pulls us within our hearts and that pulls us from our minds. Let the cries from inside us be heard across the land. Let the pervasive veil be pulled back and seen for what it truly is. An illusion. It is an illusion of the mind and of the ego. It is an illusion of the stories that have been told over and over again. It is the Truth that lies in wait. The Truth that there is no more suffering to be had because Heaven on Earth already exists. It already resides in our hearts and in our Souls. The door has already been opened to the wonder and awe that our Souls know and remember. Be true to this knowing and all will be well. For the mind can be such a powerful tool when we choose to see what we see. Do we see a cup half full or half empty? Or maybe we see the cup. The perfect cup, the chalice that holds such pure wonderment of Life and all its keepings.

Remember and recall to serve. To serve the Light that lives and dwells within you. Ask not the mind and what it thinks. Ask not the mind where and how you should move next. Ask the Light with you and sit and await the answer, the call. Allow your intuition to guide you like never before. Seek me out on the darkness of your mind. Where the doubt and fear live. Tell me what your mind is saying and give it over to me. Pray and meditate and I will guide you further along the shore of your Soul than you would ever find on your own. Take rest in my breast. Take rest in my salvation. Trust me to show you and to guide you. Trust every little bread-crumb I give you. Trust the dreams I send to you so that you start to move and align with them. Allow them to awaken your Soul from its slumber. Allow your dreams to taunt you and tease you so that you can know the greatest life that you are destined to live.

As we sit, we sit. We sit and tune into all that is you. We sit and tune into not all that you are not. You are not darkness, you are Light. You are made up of Earth, Wind, Fire and Water. You are not who you think you are and you are who you think you are. You are here to serve more greatly than you think and know. You are here to serve more deeply and greatly than all of those before you.

Yes, I speak of the scribe. For she knows not her power, her influence, her Light, her channel, her fre-quency and her Love. She has a Love so deep for all of humanity and its suffering. Even within the deep collec-tive shadows of humanity that she carries, as you all carry. Let her lead. Follow her Soul. Follow her Wind and Air, for *she* knows. She knows and understands a lot more that she is willing to portray. Do not dumb her down with your idealizations of humanity. Do not steal her from her path, her Soul's calling. Her Soul's mission. Give her Ease and give her Grace. Let her Be. Let her Shine and let her sing her happy little song. For this is a bird that is ready to take flight into realms you do not yet know. She carries her own unique frequency all unto its own. Those who know her and who have been touched by her know it. They feel it and have been caressed by it at a Soul level.

So let her lead and guide you for I lead and guide her. Let all of the guidance and wisdom I share with her be infused into your Soul. Know that this is no mistake, that you are here now, reading this, and that she is here now, writing and scribing for me, for us. For all of us are One, you see. Feel it in her in her presence. You will feel seen and heard if you give her space to shine and shine on. Do not dull her patina with your ego's needs and desires. Support her. Lift her up and let her rise. As I rose, she rises, we all rise. We need leaders to help us rise. We all need people to shine the flashlight into the darkness when we have lost our way—even those times when we know not we are lost. For it is those times when we must and shall push on. It is those times when we know it is time for all around us to take rest. To wait for us to rest and repair for a new day of higher vibrations, meaning a feel-better feeling. Wouldn't we all like that? So let not the distractions discard you from your work, from your Soul's mission and your Soul's calling.

Now is the time to let all your words shine in Life, in art, in words and in sync. In sync with your heart and all that it feels and all that it wants to know. Be true to the inherent knowledge and wisdom that your heart knows and pulses. Be true to the inherent knowledge and wisdom that your Soul knows. That this Life is an illusion of lies and misdemeanors. Meaning to not take life too seriously and to not take the illusion seriously. That is the Buddha way, the middle way. Paying your bills, keeping up with responsibilities at work and at home. Taking the garbage out. Didn't someone once say, cleanliness is next to Godliness?

Download Sixteen

My beloved children, fear not that you cannot do this, for you have me. Fear not that the naysayers will take from you all the passion and desire that you have to make this world a better place, for they will not. Fear not that their fears will encumber you, for they will not. Fear not that people do not understand, for eventually they will. Fear not that "a man" has come here today to take from you, for he has not. He only takes from himself. He only sees what he wishes to see. He only sees that which keeps him safe. He will not allow his heart to know the Divine, for the Divine had let him down, once upon a time. He does not yet understand that the

Divine was perhaps saving him from something far worse in the end. The hand of God will intervene if he/she sees that we are going astray with our gift of free choice and free will. God will interfere, if you will, to ensure that we do not go astray too much. For we all have a purpose. We all have a destiny. Do not sell yourself short on your destiny. Remember the fire in your belly to make a difference in this world. Remember how it feels to be on point. Remember how it feels to feel small and safe. Like there is something missing. Give not away your power. Give not away your garden, for we are all gardeners of Spirit, just in different ways and in different forms. Do not give into the fear of others, for it will just slow you down. Stay True to your heart and all its keepings. Stir water into wine with the alchemy that lives inside you.

Take your Spiritual gifts and share them. Share them across the land for those in need. In such deep need. They are suffering. They are dying. They are making way for you as they need you to share with them your Light and your gifts. This is not about making money per se. The money will come each day if you are sharing on point what you are called to share. So write and share what inspires you. Create ideas and share what inspires you. If Spiritual Freedom inspires you then share that. If Love inspires you, then share that. If walking dogs inspires you, then do that. Allow what ever inspires your heart to move you through Life.

Make this life yours. Not anyone else's. Make it yours. It has been given to you to make with it what you will. Do not allow anyone else's priorities to pull you or sway you from your Spiritual purpose or mission. Choose well, choose wisely. If someone contracts you too much, either physically, energetically or Spiritually, then you must make a decision. To free your Self from such constraints or to let your Self be held in a less accountable state. For at the end of the day, you are accountable to your Self and your greater power. This Life, your Life, is a gift. Use it wisely. Share it wisely. Smile. Make amends. Send good wishes. Use your heart and its wisdom wisely.

Stay on track and stay on task and all will be well. For Life supports those that are in the flow of their higher purpose, that is to say, their Divine purpose. Let not the distractions deter you from your higher calling for that is of the utmost importance. Keep yourself grounded in your positive earthly ego and all will be well. You need your ego to serve. The ego is not a Spiritual swear word. We need the ego to identify with ideas and Truths that resonate. We are here to experience Life through the Divine and we are here to let the Divine experience Life through us. What a beautiful symphony for them both to dance together, in unison, in tandem. Like two should, holding hands, dancing in the Light. For the Light will guide you and the Light will show you. It will show you the way to your deepest inner Truth. That you are Love and you came from Love. Always remember.

Always breathe and always receive.

Download Seventeen

Today, things have shifted. They have shifted greatly. The boundaries are setting you free and were holding you too tight. Someone else's boundaries were suffocating you and your new boundaries have set you free. You had dreams and they were squashed without remorse and without true regret. People help us paint our dreams and then they at times help them to evaporate. Or do they? Do you let someone take *your* dream away because they don't want to create it with you? Or do you stand tall and reclaim that gift again for your Self? Do you plant another seed of hope in your consciousness? Allow your dreams and hopes to be seen, felt and heard. Do not shy away from them. You already are abundance and you already are prosperous. Look at all of the overlooked abundance around you. Light, air, water, trees, grass, breath, food, shelter, clothing, insight, knowledge, tools, technology, etc. Do you see? You are *so* abundant in *so* many things. So, I invite you to change your mindset soon, to help you attract in more abundance than you already have.

If you shift your vibration from lack to abundance, watch your life unfold more beautifully than you have ever seen before. Allow your mind to bef, free of what it thinks abundance looks like. Is your idea of abundance the balance of your bank account or how big your house is? Or how flashy your car is? That was once believed to be true in the '80s and still is today. But as consciousness changes, we change too. Our ideas change, our beliefs change. Our world changes. Would you like more change? Then wrap yourself in the idea and notion that you *are* abundance. That every cell of your being vibrates in abundance. You have an abundance of choice each and every day from what you eat to what you wear, to how you act. Do you see? Abundance is everywhere, reflecting to you that you are abundance too. Can you feel how successful you are now at seeing your own abundance? It is all around you. Breathe. Believe. Receive.

Allow the mind to be free of the idea of diminishing returns, for what you put forward in life you will always get back tenfold. So be mindful, be playful, let loose and let in joy. If you put forward Compassion, be warned—you will receive tenfold that Compassion in return. If you put forward Peace, then it is Peace you will find. If you put forward well-wishes, then it is well-wishes you will receive. Stay true to your high heart. Stay true to its Truth, that all is well and all will be well.

Life will throw you a curve ball at times and you must learn to navigate the new terrain with as much Ease and Grace as possible. Be more gentle on yourselves and then you shall be more gentle on others. Stay true to what you believe and know to be true. Trust your intuition. Stand tall. Stand firm. Stand in your Truth. Summon greatness from your Self and others will return that greatness in kind. Summon the all that is you from inside and those around you shall and will be inspired and follow suit. Lean back and wait. Lean back and allow your Self to receive Life fully and completely. See what Life can surprise you with. Be patient. Be generous and be kind. Again, with your Self first, and then you practice these virtues with others.

Anger will arise and it can feel confusing at times. Follow the anger and you will find hurt and pain. Usually an emotional pain that runs so deep inside as though it is an open wound, constantly flowing, like a river. This river runs through our entire being and this pain will splash out sometimes in the form of anger lashing out. But to be totally and completely vulnerable is a strange place for most. It is a dark, difficult and challenging place to be, to live and to breathe. But inside these pains are so many gifts if we could just trust them to the Light. If you could just trust that the Light will bring Light to them. These burdens will become lighter, for a problem shared is a problem halved. So share. Be true to your heart. Share your vulnerabilities with a friend or family member. Offer back a compassionate ear and see what unfolds. The Truth can be a harbinger of death, in a good way. For death means transition and transitions are a wonderful thing when we can celebrate the birth of some new butterfly wings.

Download Eighteen

Let the Truth be known that you are the change maker and that you are the Truth seeker. That also means that you are a hell-raiser—in a very literal way. That your ways, your movements, your thoughts and your ideas are here—and you are here to "raise hell." Meaning to lift the veil of a false hell that we all live under at times.

You are here to make a difference. You are here to *be* the difference. Allow your Self to conjure up ideas that will make the world a better place. Allow your Self to invite and ignite ideas and ways to better the planet and humanity. Allow your imagination to fly free in the wake of uncertainty. Allow your ideas to come to life with certainty, clarity and Valour. Allow your intentions to fly free. Allow your energy to rise into your high heart. Allow your Spirit to soar. Allow your heart to be free. Allow your heart to pour forth in all its courage and Valour. Allow your voice to be heard. Allow your heart to sing. Allow your tune to shine in the stars and allow your chanting to call out into the wild of the night and effuse the elusive hearts to *rise*. Allow your breath to light up the night with the word. Allow all of your glory to be about you and your mission, your purpose, your passion, your Spiritual inheritance. Your bounty. Your glory.

See not the mistake that the mind makes mistakes. For a mistake is a mis-take. Is there really such a thing? Yes, there is, but very few. Allow the mis-takes that you think and feel are mistakes to anchor you more deeply in the present moment. Allow *all* of *your* mis-takes to guide you home to your Soul's journey. Allow your Self to be One with the Divine and the path it has for you.

Allow your mind to be free from all that it wants to deter you from. Allow you heart to be totally free. Free to feel. Free to Love. Free to Love *all* in a healthy way. In a God Way. Not in a selfish way. Not in a way that feeds your mind but robs your Soul. In a way that bears good fruit. In a way that bears your name. Your signature. That is what the world needs right now. It needs you. Humanity needs you. They need you. To lay down your doubts to rest and follow me.

Allow me to show you the way forward. A way forward to a new humanity where there lives *so* much Ease and Grace. It is so close you can taste it, can't you? You understand that all it truly takes is one small shift. A shift into *true* Love and Compassion. A shift into the true Truth. A shift into a place that no one has been before, except in their dreams. This is *the* new world that is already here. She is already upon us and in us. We are now just igniting the hearts to the Light that already lives inside them. To the Light of Higher Knowing and to a Light of Higher Wisdom. And it is Higher. It is Higher in vibration. It is Higher in awareness because it comes from "On High."

So trust your intuition. Trust *our* intuition and let me show you how the world can be with your assistance. Allow me to take you by the hand and show you how we are all here for the same purpose. To rise in Love and Compassion in a deeper way that has never been done before. And that includes allowing those who must fall to fall. For when they fall, then they must Rise. And they will either choose to Rise to the Heaven in their hearts while in their bodies or Rise to a Heaven outside themselves, outside their bodies. We are all here as bodhisattvas.

Download Nineteen

Today there is a new energy in the air. It's the energy of Trust, in a whole new way you have never seen or felt before. Allow and Trust are the words for today. Let your heart be clear. Let your mind be clear. Let the Truth unfold before you. Know that what you see and feel is coming. Know that what you see and feel is unfolding. Know that the scars that you have are indeed to your beautiful. Know that the scars in your mind are being lifted. Know that there is no more reason to look back over your shoulder and second-guess, to second judge or to fix or heal any more. You are perfect and beautiful just the way you are in the eyes of God and the Divine. Trust me that that is Truth. Trust me that that is the knowing that I have deep inside my heart that I share with you on this day. Trust me that I hold the keys to your future, just allow me to show you and guide you for it is my honor. Trust me to show you the way and just keep breathing. Allow me to lead you by the hand with a blindfold over your eyes.

I understand and know how this can feel fateful at times. And it is. But in such a beautiful way, you have no idea the Glory and the Heaven that lies in wait for you. All of the shadows you have worked on are now in the Light and you have embraced every single one of them. That is the work and now you are done. So sit back, listen, breathe and receive. It's all happening. It's all unfolding.

Let the Truth in your heart unfold to the deeper knowing inside your High Heart. The High Heart is the Spiritual Heart and it is the way home. It is the way home to the salvation that lives in your High Heart. Not the salvation that you have come to believe or know, but the salvation that will truly save you from your Self. You see, what if suffering is an illusion and we are all crucifying ourselves? That is a bold question and statement but I offer it as a healing balm to your confusions, to your maladies, to your woes and to your follies.

What if we could stand together and I could show you how to see the world through rose-colored glasses. Would that interest you? What if I told you that this is all an illusion. Would that change your mind about Life and how you experience it? What if I told you that what you see is not true? That what you hear is not true and that what you touch is not true? Meaning, what if I told you that all of your senses have been corrupted except your sense of smell? What if I told you that your mind has you *so* programmed in the wrong way that it is dis-serving and un-serving you. What if told you I know a secret way out of all of this suffering. Would you choose it? Would you be curious to try and truly heal your Self once and for all? Does that sound nice? Does that feel good? Does it sound appealing? I would imagine your answers would be yes.

So let's begin a new day...now.

The Earth is round, yes? Not flat, agreed?

So why do you spend so much time worrying about the climate? If Earth is a self-contained sphere, she will never run out of water, as she is constantly in a state of recycling. We must trust the evolution and the intelligence of the planet. She has outlived any of us *ever* and will continue to do so. She is a living, breathing being that science does not accept for. Science does not account for the Spirit of our Beautiful Mother Earth, yet there is a continuous bashing about her deficiencies and her future.

I am here to tell you it is false. The conclusions are false, because they do not take into account the vast Intelligence of the Universe and the Universal design. We hold the key to the future. Meaning, we, the Spiritual Wisdom Keepers, hold a deeper knowing of the future and what the Earth will look like and be like. You cannot imagine it beyond our wildest senses. She is evolving into a Garden of Eden for all of you to play in and rejoice in. Allow your Self to even imagine this right now, or feel it in your body, which is even better.

The illusion is this. That humans hold the destiny of the planet in their hands. They actually don't. She does. Meaning Earth. She is a Sovereign Being and she knows her destiny. But our dear Mother Earth is waiting for something. She is waiting for us to remember who we are and where we came from. Some people call this waking up. We call it *remembering*, for you are always awake on some level. We are so excited at this time to watch, listen and guide you all. For there are so many of us here, helping you, showing you and guiding you.

Allow some time to ponder this. Allow your heart to take in all of the magic that the Earth has to offer. Allow your Self to see the plants differently. Allow your Self to listen to our Divine Mother Earth and see her for the beautiful Being that she is. Allow your Self to be drunk on the wine of her beauty. Eat from the Earth. Eat wholesome food. Try to redeem all of the synthetic food that exists to nothing. Allow your body to breathe more deeply on the inside with fresh oxygenated food. Keep eating the greens, for they are good for the blood. Keep drinking the pure water, for it flushes and purifies the skin and organs. Keep smelling the roses, as they hold the highest vibration of all flowers and the scent is pure Heaven. Keep connected with your pets and animals as they are way-showers to guide us back into our hearts. Help to alleviate their suffering in any way you can. Say no to leather, eat more meatless meals. Show Compassion for their life, for they matter too. There is plenty of nutrition on Mother Earth, in all of her bounty. This does not have to be a perfect practice, but every effort counts. A proverbial drop in the ocean.

Every conscious effort expands and multiplies energetically. The expression "no good deed goes unpunished" no longer serves. It is a falsehood. Let's eradicate this saying. How you ask? When someone says anything negative, we retaliate with *more* kindness. We bring the strongest antidote we know. We bring Love and Compassion. We ask, "what do you mean by that?" in a gentle voice and a kind heart. We ask and then we listen. We ask again and then we listen some more. And if you find that there is a finger being pointed at one of your faults, you "own it". You take *full* responsibility for your words, actions and attitudes. You act and become the bigger person.

Yet, protect and remove your Self from any abuse or false accusations. Politely excuse your Self from the conversation and the energy flowing toward you will stop. Your actions will speak far louder than any words you see, as our hearing has been corrupted. So, please, with Grace, remove your Self from any conversation that might be accusatory. Remember that the mind likes to make a lot of assumptions and that goes both ways— for you when you are listening, and for your counterpart when someone else is sharing.

Download Twenty

Today is the glory of a new day. Each day you wake is a day full of endless possibilities. Each day is full of renewal. Each day is full of wonderful and ecstatic potential. Each day is full of you. You are the new beginning. You are the Grace to make things easier for others. You are the Divine tool that is being used to bring more Peace and healing to the planet. You are the embodiment of a bodhisattva in true form. You are the Yin to the Yang. You are the bloom to the flower and the crow to the cry. You are the polarity to your Self in a way that nobody is yet quite here to understand. You are here to make a huge difference and you are here to change lives. So please stand tall and stand firm in your convictions that you know best. For the way that you know inside your heart is best. The way to a better place and a better Earth is inside your heart. Inside to the places that hurt, to the places that need healing and to the places that we call home when our hearts are wide open in full expression of our Divine nature.

Allow your Self some time and space to breathe and to take it all in. Allow your Self some time and space to let things shift and settle. Rome was not built in a day. So take the time, perhaps a day, to sit in Gratitude and receive. Sit and receive all of the blessings and the abundance around you before you push onward and upward. Breathe, believe and receive. It's all happening.

Trust the flow and things will flow. When we don't trust the flow, things will not flow. So stand more free and stand more tall and all will be well. Notice when you are staying small, you are "playing small". Notice when you stand tall your energy shifts. People might notice you more. What they notice is your energy. What they feel is your energy. They feel your certainty and confidence and they in part would like to know how to arrive there with you.

They want to feel how you feel. They want to feel the certainty that you feel. They want to stand tall as you do. We shrug our shoulders because of shame and we shrug our shoulders to protect our hearts. When they hurt, we tend to shy away and turn away to protect our hearts. This is a normal human tendency that one can understand. And I invite you to always remember that your heart is made of pure gold because it is made of Spirit. So no one can ever completely break your heart. It may feel like it at times, but you survive, you pull through, because of the Light that dwells inside you.

People can be tough. Their behaviors can be rough. But allow Grace time and time again to move through you. Practice forgiveness. Practice Grace. Practice Ease. Practice your Practice. Go now. Stop here. Practice your practice.

Download Twenty-One

Let us be moved by the power within. Let us be moved by the Light within. Let us grow far beyond anyone can imagine in their minds and in their hearts. Let us press forward with our faces to the wind. Let us lean into whatever makes us uncomfortable. Let us find a way within that makes us feel like we don't have to go without. Let us be free in our hearts to Love in such deep ways, we cry. Let us Love in such deep ways, we weep. Let us Love in such deep ways, we laugh. And let us Love in such deep ways we move in Bliss and Joy. That we breathe in Bliss and Joy and that we bestow Bliss and Joy onto those that we meet. Not by our words, but just by our presence.

Let us allow ourselves to be moved. Let us allow ourselves to be freed. To be freed from ourselves. Let ourselves be moved from our fears. Let ourselves be moved by Grace. Let ourselves be moved by Love. Let ourselves be moved by all that is and all that shall be. Let ourselves be infused with the energy that flies off these pages. Let ourselves be free from the stirrings and the distractions of the mind. Let ourselves be free from the doubt of others. Let ourselves be free from the mundane. For God did not bring you here to live a Life of the mundane.

You were brought here to have the Light move through you. You were brought here to have the Essence of Spirit paint the world through your hand. You were brought here on a bed of roses, but it is understood at times, you only feel the thorns. The crucifixion is real, the crucifixion is true. The crucifixion tells a tale of Truth. The crucifixion that I chose on some level was to invite great change, but not in the ways that you all thought and have come to believe. I bled on *that* cross on *that* day so that people would take notice. I bled for the resurrection of Love and Compassion.

I bled so that people would feel my pain and my Glory. I bled so that people could feel their own pain and their own Glory. I bled so that people would and could feel again. We had become a nation, a people, a country where Love had run out. Love had run out of the hearts of humanity and My Father called me to the cross to set things anew. Let this Truth move through you. Let your body tell the Truth of my words. Allow your heart to guide you to your True North, to the compass inside your heart that tells which way is left and which way is right. I implore you to choose the straight path. I implore you to choose the middle way.

I implore you to listen to my scribe, for she too has been crucified like me over and over, and this is why I have chosen her for this *huge* undertaking. For she has learned through Grace, hard work, Trust and practice to infuse herself with my Love over and over and over, even when Life has thrown her off the proverbial horse. Even when Life has thrown her out of her own family again and again, she Rises each and every time with a warm, giving and generous heart where she can. For she too has a human Life she must manage. For she too has a human heart that she must decode. For she, too, has been laid on a cross and nailed over and over again. For she too has lain her heart down for me even in her triumph and tribulations. For she has seen, felt and experienced a crucifixion repeatedly in her darkest hours. She has battled depression with a Grace I have never seen before. She has battled abuse with such Grace, she has been bestowed a Purple Heart. She has been picked on and picked over in such a way, you would recoil at the scene if you could know it. She has been given a path. She has been given a journey, without any religious or Spiritual upbringing to support her in her darkest hours and doubt, betrayal and continued abuse. Yet she has, time and time again, sought my Love, sought me to show her and to guide her even when she has no proof of my Love for her. Just a deep knowing in her blood and in her bones that there is a force, there is something bigger that is driving her and holding her as the delicate and pungent flower that she is.

So, I invite you to step back and breathe. I invite you to step back and devour the pages of this book. Let them pour into your heart. Let them pour into your being. Let them fill you and your cup up. Let them runneth over. Let them runneth over your heart and your mind as you cast the doubts away. Let them pour over onto you as you cast aside the negativity, the doubt, the fears and the loss.

For the loss has made you much freer than you can ever know. The loss has gifted you a certain freedom from attachment. This is one of the gifts of loss. To free us from the ideas that we are attached to things in ways we are not. To be attached to outcomes. To be attached to endings. To be attached is to be normal. And then we must let go. To be attached to our thoughts is to drain our energy field of all its pure potential. To be attached to the flow of your work, your calling...now that is a beautiful thing. To be attached to the outcome of those you share your Love with, now that is wondrous. Like a child that sets the balloon free unto the sky and can't help but watch it take flight. Like a mother that nudges her fledglings out of her nest.

There is a time in nature and there is a time within us. There is also a time in humanity where there is nowhere for us to go but forward. To lean in, to push on, to remember why we are here. To enjoy the fruits of our labor and to share those fruits with others. To allow a clearer and Lighter breath of Life to be shared and harnessed across the land. To go within and find your Truth. To go without and find your Truth. To go outside and find your Truth. For the Truth is all around you if you choose to see it through the eyes of Love. The Truth lives deep within you if you choose to stand in the eyes of Love. The Truth shall set you free if you allow your Self to move. The Truth shall be One with you if you allow it. The Truth will always find you if you let it. The Truth will always know you if you let it see you.

Give into the pullings in your heart. Trust that they are guiding you to just the right place. The right place that stands true and that stands tall must be felt in that sacred place that dwells right there, deep within the throne of your heart. Deep within the sacred temple of the heart. Deep within the heart of the name of Jesus and of Love and Compassion. His teachings are these. Nothing more, nothing less.

To be a citizen of humanity, including animals, is to be a citizen of the heart. To be a law-abiding citizen if that law is built upon democracy and does not take anyone's human rights away.

Always question. Always ask questions. Boundaries are good and necessary to move populations and then when do human rights take over? And if human rights do take over, who carries that bloodshed? Should it be those you hath forsaken or shall it be those who are already enjoying such greats fruits from their own hard work?

Shall there be such a place where one decides from another their future and their fate? Shall a human freedom be a Spiritual Gift that all of humanity gets to receive and actualize? If the answer is yes, then how *do* we make this happen? If the answer is yes, then how *do* we make this known? If the answer from your heart is yes, then how *do* we ensure that this happens? If the answer is yes, then how *do* we open people's hearts and minds further into a realm they do not even know exists inside their hearts?

Download Twenty-Two

The day is upon us. The day of Peace is upon us for it dwells deep within your heart and within mine. The day has come where you and I align to Life's highest good and that is Peace. Imagine if all beings felt at Peace? Imagine if all beings only felt True un-conditional Love. There would be no more need to hurt or injure others. There would be no more need to take from others and we would live in a far more generous heart and Spirit. But alas, that vision only for now lives with so many hearts of humanity. But how do we make it real? How do make this manifestation real? We start by believing. We start by being. We start by acting as though it is already done. We give Gratitude for the Peace that will soon prevail across the planet. That is how we anchor Peace. We become it. This is how we anchor all, we become it. If we want happiness, we become it. If we want Love, we become it. If we want Peace, we become it.

I invite you to tell all of your Loved Ones. Tell them… shout it from the rooftops! *If you want peace you must become it!* Tell everyone you know and we can continue the movement that Gandhi created. If we want Peace, we *must* become it.

Let those who are not interested fall away and bless them. Respect their path but do not allow it to deter you from yours. Envelop your self with the unconditional Love that the Divine has for you, and then share that with those around you, whom you Love. Show them the way. Show them the deeper way to the Truth of the Light and to the Truth of Divinity. That Love rules the Kingdom of Heaven and that we *can* create Heaven on Earth. We do not need to donate Love, but we can give it away freely. Give it to all of those you Love and adore and Bless those that make it difficult for you to Love and adore. For they are the ones that need your Love and attention the most. They are the ones that need the affection of your heart the most.

Be true to what your heart tells you. Be true to what you heart hears and be true to what your heart wants. Be true to all that you want to manifest no matter what the proverbial price.

Your heart matters. Your wishes matter. Your desires and wants matter. Allow your Self to be moved. Allow your Self to be moved by the force of God, Love and Light. Allow your Self to be freed by the concepts of the mind. And give yourself permission to be freed by your heart. Give yourself permission to be given all that you wish for. Allow your Self to receive, even though this is uncomfortable at times. Allow your Self to be and sit comfortably with all that is. Allow your Self to see your patterns of where you cannot and do not receive. For all that lies in wait is all of the forms of all of the abundance you wait for.

Do you know that it is you who keeps it at arms length? Do you know that it is you who keeps it a distance away? Do you know that the reason you do this is because you believe you are not worthy? Because you believe that you are not worth the gold that you are? It is because you see your Self and believe your Self to be separate from source, from God, from Love and from Light. But you are Light. You came from the Light. *You are the Light*. You are the Divine walking. You are the Divine running and you are the Divine Incarnate. You are God because you came from God. This is what Oneness means. To embrace the Light in you, and then you can embrace it and see it in others. Allow your Self to be seen so that Life and the World can offer you a reflection of that which you do not see in your Self. Allow God and all of your Loved Ones to show you how much you are Loved. Allow your Self to receive and see all that you really are. Allow your Light to Shine. Allow your words to glow. Allow your gifts to heal those that need them. Don't they all need it? Think of how many people you have served and whose pain has stopped in some way. Think and remember all of the lost Souls who have been searching and seeking for some kind of support and you were the only one who could offer them the super specific kind of support that they needed. This is not a way that has been done and cast before. There is a new imprint. There is a new beginning and a new movement.

It does not have to be perfect for you are human as I once was. I was not always kind to my disciples. I was gruff at times. For there was a passion that fueled my passion. There was a fire in my belly that seemed like nobody would know how to understand. There are few who can touch it and understand what I feel and have felt of humanity, but the scribe whom I have chosen to share these words with you can. *She* understands in the most ways an everyday human can. My word cannot pass through someone who has given their life to service and to a church, who has had no children, who has not had to fend for themselves in a world that was full of hate and hypocrisy for a short while. But by a woman who has been crucified repeatedly. I have tested her Strength and I have tested her Faith. I have tested her psychologically, emotionally and physically with pain so great, most would not pass. She has persevered and served. She has come undone and then rewired herself. She has been tormented but still gives with a warm smile. She has succumbed to all the pain and has still found God in all of it, where most would not. She is a brave Soul who needs not much. For she hears the whispers of my heart and of yours.

Let her show you and guide you for she is My Truth. Let her unravel your heart and show you the way to the deeper Truth that lives inside you. Let her shine your spiritual shoes. Let her mid-wife your Soul. Let her peel off your mask and help you to see the real you.

She is a great Soul and a great wisdom keeper who understands more than she reveals. There is a twinkling inside her that you will be hard-pressed to find in anyone else. Her gifts that I share with her to share with you are extra-ordinary. Her ability to see the unseen is finite. Her Grace, which she uses to comprehend when to share and when not to share, is so clear. Her understanding of the sacredness of her gifts and her service is Divine. So I ask you to trust in me that I have given you into the arms of her. Please trust her as you do me. Please follow her heart as she follows mine. She will be a wonderful medium and translator for the work that is to be done on this one home we call Earth. So, I also ask you to give her some room to breathe and all will be well. Give her some room to shine and all will be well. Give her some room to sparkle and to fill a room with that sparkle and all will be well. For, *I have* chosen her as my messenger and she has deserved to become my messenger as I have tested here again and again and through and through.

I repeat...you will not find another like her with all of her wisdom and Grace. You may seek, but you will not find another who embodies a frequency like mine. Even Priests do not, but they do find her interesting...because she energetically and Spiritually carries the code. The code of Love and Compassion and Wisdom and Grace. Fear not what your mind is trying to tell you right now. Fear not the way in which this is all unfolding is such a non-traditional way. But you see, history must not repeat itself, for that is where the failure lies. The failure lies in the old traditions of fear teachings and controlling and shaming humanity with their own shadows. The failure lies in believing a scripture that was written 300 years beyond its time. There lives not undeniable proof of the allegories, yet I will share with you this at this time. *Now* it the time to leave that all behind and to start anew. This scribe is a new disciple, if you will. A disciple of Love. And this new scripture, if you will, is just that. A new scripture. It is a new way of being. It is a new way of being with a higher vibration. This is why the cover is gold and white. These two colors hold the highest vibration spiritually. As does the Rose...specifically the Red Rose that adorned the first book written by the scribe.

But her legacy is this...

To have and to hold and to leave this planet, when it is her time, a better place. A wiser place. A kinder place and a more playful place. So that *all* of the children (young and old) will feel free enough to play hard at whatever they want to play at. Do you see? The anticipation of the second coming actually created so much fear, because some believed a nation of sorts would die. That those not willing to believe in the Christ would suffer an immeasurable death and afterlife.

Nothing could be further from the Truth. Death dies each day only to be reborn. Your Spirit never dies. It can't. You are always connected to the One True Source. That is what is meant by the illusion, in a way. That is why we suffer and crucify ourselves. It is because you are in this world, but not of it. It is because you are a part of Life but not about it. Life is about you and about everything around you *and* it is a reflection of you. That is the new wave of One Consciousness. Now

I ask you to ride the wave with me. So, what if suffering is an illusion and we are only crucifying ourselves? What if we can change the wave of consciousness we are currently in? What if we have admitted to ourselves that we are beyond all that we can measure? How do you measure your Spirit? How do you measure your Soul? How do you measure your Intentions? How do you measure your Love? You can't. But you can feel these things. So how do we measure feelings? We can't, and we do know that they can feel big and small at times.

So, come, child of mine.

Sit down with me and relax. Give way to that huge heart inside you that knows no bounds. Meaning the heart inside you that lives and dwells in Unconditional Love. Yes… it is there. It is Compassion and it is Kindness. All you can do is offer a branch. If some do not wish to partake and hold the branch, then that is their choice, but not my will for them. For their will, when it struggles against my will, is what creates the suffering you see. So trust, allow me to show you and allow me to guide you… all the way. I know that the waters will get tough at times and that someone else's will might try as to get in the way. But here I am. I will lead you and where I am, please follow. Trust in your Higher Power. The Higher Power of Love, Light and Life. That is what I ask of you and that is what I will show you, dear one. Please take my hand. Place the other hand over your heart and breathe. Feel and know that I am with you 100 percent of the way. If at times you feel like you are in the darkness, just close your eyes and reach for my hand and you shall find my comfort, my strength and my knowings that you are beyond this world.

Yes, you are human, but know also that you are beyond *this*. You are to live beyond this time and this space here on Earth. You live and dwell beyond, in a place where no one has limits and everyone is free. Their liberation has been realized and actualized and it is oh so beautiful. So, please know that every door you find that is locked, and every bridge you are asked to cross over, is a way to more deeply discover the Divine within your Self and to see it and feel it within everyone else.

Take back your Life from those who have stolen it. Take back your dignity from those who have robbed it from you: including your Self. Take back your pride and embrace that your humanity has standards. Heed not those that want to Spiritually whitewash things as karmic or past life credit or debt. We are moving beyond that, dear Soul. We are entering a time of liberation and freedom.

Download Twenty-Three

Today there has been a coming of sorts. A coming of a deeper Truth that the world is ready to align with. Humanity is working oh so hard to ward off any further injury to itself. You will see this in people as they bite the hand that feeds them because they believe they are undeserving. They will try and brainwash you into fear. They will paint lines as boundaries but they only become borders for themselves that keep people out. The people they keep out the most are the people they need the most. For they are Compassion, they are Kindness and they embody Oneness.

It is this Oneness that has these people gripping at their throats in fear. It is this Oneness that they long to feel but keep it away out of fear of losing themselves. It is the fear of losing themselves that creates more fear, so there is pattern of holding. Holding themselves up against themselves. Not breathing, not bending, not stretching for that would stretch the mind too much and this can feel too threatening to the ego. Yoga has become so popular in the last few decades in pop culture to aid in the infusing of a flexible mindset. A flexible body creates a flexible mind, and vice versa.

Poll all of those around you and ask them if they would like to have a more flexible mind. Most people would scrunch up their noses and seem confused by the question. Most people's egos feel very threatened of you trying to change their status quo. Actually, if you try and change it at all, they will try and keep their fears from you. Underneath, the higher part of them knows they are holding on to them too tightly because of fear. They will try and put it off as nothing. As just the news they are listening to, without truly understanding that that particular news they choose to watch is a reflection of their mindset and with the main networks it is usually a very negative one. What you watch on television and at the movies shows you where you are vibrating. What music you listen to shows where you are vibrating.

So, with encouragement: Be more mindful. Be more considerate. Be more playful. Stretch your ears. Try new things. Try new sounds. Get with the times and don't stay stuck in the past. Be fully present with the world going on around you. Men, take heed: Women can run countries, companies and families without your presence. What does this tell you about the state of man? A lot, but that is for another day.

Believe in the Oneness that I am speaking of. There is a Oneness inside you that is dying to be seen and to be heard. There is a Oneness inside that *knows* what your mission is and your goals are. If you are aligned with your most authentic Self, then your mission and your goals will be the same. If you have not a mission of your heart, then your goals will seem far-reaching and will elude you, for they come from the ego. The ego is not a negative thing. It is needed for survival. It stops you from stepping out in front of a bus. But if the ego prevents you or others from being in your heart, then it has become a problem. For the ego is a collection of ideas, beliefs and defense mechanisms mostly programmed into you by age seven. If the defense mechanisms are too strong, then it will be challenging to change the ingrained ideas and beliefs of the world, humanity and Life.

The unwillingness to change these are what keeps us stuck and stagnant. For if there is no growth, the Soul will start to wilt. Depression might set in. Weight gain might set it. Self-loathing might set in. But fear not, for the Soul will always seek to grow, bend and stretch toward the Light. This is one of the reasons yoga is so much enjoyed. It is a workout for the Soul—but we won't tell the ego that, for it might resist.

So, with all of this in hand: Free your mind. Free your heart and free your hate. Allow others to be who they chose to be. Give up trying to control how they see you and what they think of you. You are worth more than that. Find your tribe that adores you and Loves you for who you are. Surround your Self with those that nurture you and who support you authentically. Let go of any and all expectations that they should be different from who they are, for that is what holds you prisoner. You see, this shows you where your own personal beliefs get in the way. The belief that things should be different. The belief that things should be better. The belief that everyone will want to and should grow as you do. Do you see the expectation and demand that you are holding over others? Let people be how they are. Hold a space in your heart for Love either near or far, without judgments. They are beating to their own drum and they have every right to do that. They can make whatever music they want and dance to it however they wish, as long as they are not stepping on or breaking your toes. If it feels like they are, then it is time for you to find another dance partner. No harm or no foul. Just two beautiful souls with conflicting needs. One might need respect while the other needs full-time attention. One neither less nor more—just different.

Can you find the Peace in that? Can you remove the rantings of the mind and the polarization that happens when you part ways with a Beloved or a friend? Let the other be the other and you be you. Don't try to change the perceptions someone has of you, for they have their own filters, their own layers of experiences and self-judgments that they will project onto you. Only an awakened and Truly empowered person will know and understand this as the way of the complex human heart.

This Soul will understand how we are all here guided by Spirit, and that there is a "Father" of sorts guiding us and holding us each step of the way. So do not play small to keep the other safe. Do not give up on your dreams just because "they" think their dreams are more lively or more important. Ask your Self: "What are *my* dreams?" Find a pen and paper and write them down.

Download Twenty-Four

Today you have come undone in a beautiful way. In a way that makes your Soul laugh and giggle, for it is coming to know and to understand more deeply why you are here and why we are all here. It is to learn. It is to grow. It is to evolve. It is to show your Self and those who show interest around you a way forward. It is to let your Self be who you are at all costs. It is to let your self see and be seen for the amazing and Divine human being that you are. It is to let your Light sparkle and be seen for its true Light. It is to let your Self be known by your own heart. It is to let your self be your *Self*. It is to cast away all of the underpinnings to your true essence. It is to let your true nature nurture you, and when appropriate, those around you. It is to take us back to a time of service of the heart. It is to move past our own laziness and to get up, wake up and serve.

Today, we have come closer. We are getting closer. We are getting closer to each other in our hearts and in our minds. We are beginning to encircle each other and help each other to complete each other like nobody has before. We are beginning to see and more deeply understand the you in me and the you in us. To see and feel each other as fellow human beings. To not take on each other's pain, but to lend a compassionate ear to that pain.

That is the pain that lives and dwells in nearly each and every being who is on the human path. The pain that has brought you further forth into creation. The pain that you are more and have more deeply come here to understand is yours to heal on this human journey. To know that you are two that have been Divined into one, and that it is in that oneness that you will find Oneness. That you will find it one day soon, if you have not yet already remembered your sacred Oneness with the Divine, with your Creator and with your Master.

Self-Mastery at its best. When you know that you are not your Master and at the same time you are. For you are a slice of the Divine. You are God incarnate. You are the full embodiment of Bliss and Joy and Love and Peace. That you are a manifestation of Surrender walking. Now, when you walk, walk with that Surrender. Share that vibration consciously. Let others feel it and be touched by it. Let them hear you breathe that new breath they are looking for. Let them feel your energies and your vibration under this sun on this day. Go out into the world and be one with community. Do not hide alone at home once you have found Peace. For it is your call to return that newfound Peace to community over and over again, like shepherding sheep over and over the rolling hills.

Let your newly remembered freedom be the antidote to so much suffering. Share your newly recognized way of being always. It is your duty to the Divine to be in service to the Light. To be an inspiration to all and to let those who are not interested to just pass by with a glimpse, for that alone will plant an energetic seed within them that their Higher Self will, in time, guide them too. It does not have to be nor should it be such hard work. Let those who are ready receive, and those who are not will not yet. Trust the Divine timing in all of the complexities of the matrix of Life and God's work.

Allow your heart to give a reservoir of permission to your heart to be free. You are free to Love whom you wish to Love. You are free to share friendship and Love with any friend you choose. You are a free agent to Love and all its keepings, as long as you are not crossing any boundaries that may be in agreement with someone else. Monogamy of the heart is a tricky subject. Brotherly and sisterly Love are the safest types of Love to share. It is a respectful, kind and all-Loving Love even when someone's behavior might be temporarily upsetting. This Love can find its balance again quite easily if given time and space. It is not a Love that is jealous or boastful. It is a kind Love that wants nothing but its brother or sister to be free of pain and drenched with Love at all times. For Love heals, if we let it. Love can cut through so much of the ego if we let it. Love can temper our words and our thoughts if we let it. Love can infuse the self with a deeper Self if we let it.

So…allow. Allow the healing balm of Love to soothe your aches and pains. Allow the hand of Love to caress your shoulder. Allow the kiss of Love to heal your shame. Allow the feeling of Love to find you. Allow the purest of Love, Divine Love, to wash over you and guide you to your heart's heart. For that is where your deepest Truth lies and that is where your deepest Truth Lives. In the well of your heart, in the chamber of your Sacred Heart. The place inside you where I live. The place inside you where I call you to rise and to resurrect your Self-Love and your Self-Compassion. *That* is the second coming, you see.

It is not a one-time event. It is another wave of consciousness coming upon us to wake us up even more than we already are. It is the 5D to the 3D as some of you understand it. It is the yin to the yang. It is the ebb to the flow. It is the future allegory to the parable of the past. For that past has finally arrived in the here and now. I have been resurrected in your hearts. In all of the hearts that will allow the awakening of the Christ Consciousness. It is a feeling. A knowing code. This is not for the teaching of the mind. We are now beyond that. It is a frequency that will come and has shown up as a deliverable.

Download Twenty-Five

Give your Self permission, dear one, to stand up and dust your Self off and be who you are truly are. Do not let the ogres from your past keep giving you their injuries from their past, for they are not yours to hold. They are theirs to hold. They are theirs to keep and theirs to heal. They no longer need to be in acquaintance with you if they hurt you or hurl at you any words of un-affirmation, any words that hold the denial of their true selves. For this is a prime example of ego at its purest. A super-ego if you will, that has so many strong and rigid patterns and beliefs that just do not serve anymore in this new wave of consciousness. These super-egos will try and cut you down, hold you back from your true calling and derail you from the path of Love. They will try and break your Spirit by shuttering your energy field in point-blank range. Hurling words or energies that could potentially be hurtful and certainly not helpful.

What these super-egos don't know is that you have called upon your inner super-hero to counterbalance their super-ego, and therefore they don't stand a chance. Because the inner super-hero knows that it is from the Light, and that its Light is way more powerful than the super-ego's darkness. The Light will always win because the darkness truly has no power. It only has power when we give it power. I cannot tell you more clearly than this. The darkness only has power when we give it power. To become more mindful of what power and energies you are giving away to the person who is challenged with their own darkness and shadows. They will feed off your Light energy to fill up their empty cups as they have not yet cultivated their own direct connection to source. They will energetically drain you as long as you let them.

The key is not to let them. How? By having clear and strict boundaries around what you need and what you don't need. Knowing your true self and gifting your Self the gift of not comprising any boundaries that do not align with your Soul. For example, your life's work or your Soul's purpose. Never, I repeat, never let someone come between you and your Father's business, God's work, your Divine purpose. This purpose upholds the utmost important gift and act of service you can bestow upon your Self, your Father and your community. And most of all, your warrior's heart. It is there, in that place and in this space where the sacred windows are thrown wide open. Where caution is thrown to the wind and the ego is transcended, in a way. For this is not the work of the ego, this is the work of the Soul. There is a fine quality of difference between these two places and how the work comes and evolves.

For some it may be a musical Masterpiece, for others serving their family of five. For one being a medical servant, for another being a clean waste servant. Different roles, yet all are equal in importance and value. Let the mind go away and now listen to your heart. What is your heart whispering to you? What does your heart want you to hear? What does your mind want to interrupt you with? Please do not make the error of bargaining with your Soul's purpose. For this creates a distortion in the Spiritual atmosphere and everything is connected.

I will not say that this is true but if we imagine the butterfly effect to be true, then how do we truly know that us not doing something isn't causing a change in weather patterns on the planet? As I said, everything is connected. Even earthquakes can be manifestations of energy moving in deep levels within the planet as they move deeply within ourselves.

Imagine you are flying free the way your God intended. Imagine the tethers and the chains are coming off. Imagine that the end result is freedom from all of the low vibrational energies that are so difficult to navigate being human. The shame, the guilt, the anger, the blame, the sadness, the pain of all types. This is ascension. When we, the collective we, transcend and ascend out of that.

Your scribe shared a story of an experience she had only several years ago. She witnessed, saw, felt, *very* deeply, a loved one transitioning out of his body and ascending after his physical death. She witnessed and tasted the glorious feeling of being free from of all the aforementioned human chains. And she felt envy. She felt envy at the very moment the departed Loved one ascended through three hoops of a bluish white Light. Purifying hoops. Circles of Divinity if you will. These hoops were Divinely appointed healing circles. A portal, if you will, to more freedom, more Love and more Grace. And until such a point in humanity where Love on Earth does not reflect Divine Love, then those three hoops will exist. One day it will only be two hoops, then one, then none. That is when we all anchor the frequency of Divine Love here on Earth. That is when, here on the earthly plain, war will end. Famine will end, because greed will end. Greed is the most all-encompassing of the proverbial seven deadly sins. Not to imply that the seven deadly sins are in fact deadly, for most of them are illusions. Except greed. Greed is from the darkness. It is a curse, if you will, that was imposed on humanity when Beelzebub fell from God's side. When he fell into his own darkness, he took humanity with him.

Download Twenty-Six

For today is another day. There is the supposition that you are taking your time to integrate and read all that is being shared in and on these pages. There is a frequency being delivered as we have already expressed. That frequency goes up incrementally the more you read. So rest, drink water and integrate when you can. Take time for your Self to allow your own personal tide to rise. As each personal rising tide lifts all boats, each personal win with Gratitude and Grace lifts many. Each person who proposed to you that their way was the only way was incorrect. There are many ways to do things and one system does not work for everyone, nor should it.

You are all extremely unique individuals with different belief systems, different karmic patterns, different needs and different visions. Once you have a shared vision, then there is space and time for collaboration. For collaboration is the adult version of sharing. The way we used to share when young. With our hearts open. It's time to reopen at the heart and share again, in the Spirit of collaboration. See what transpires and how one reacts when you invite them to collaborate. Hopefully, if they are willing to connect to their inner child in a healthy way, then they will feel joy at the inclusiveness of your offer. Hopefully they will respond with a resounding *yes*! Until the ego starts to think: "What's in it for me?" This can be managed or up-leveled by thinking what's in it for others. How can it serve the masses? How can this opportunity serve those who need it most? That is how we become servants of the heart.

Download Twenty-Seven

Today things are unfolding in a different way. We have come to time and place in space where all things are being turned over in a way. This turning over that you have felt is a turning of the tide within one's self. It is a turning over of things in a new way. This new way is the new *now* that you have been waiting for. And the new *now* that you have been searching for. This is now and the time is now. The time is now for all things to be let go of that are simply no longer serving you at a Soul level. For the work and the path that you have come here to explore and to be in Divine service to is asking that of you. It is asking for your complete will to be guided toward the Light of God. It is asking for the Light in your heart to turn toward integrity. It is asking that the Light in you be a guide for others to find the Light. To find the Truth of the path and to find complete integrity moving forward. It is there in that place where more lights get turned on inside the hearts of humanity. It is there where more integrity and authenticity is found. So turn your Light so brightly that it blinds, and then allow others to follow it when they adjust to this new Light. It is a new path you are illuminating for them. Be bold, be brave. Go forth in fortitude, strength and resolve that this is the better way and the higher way for all. Trust the call in your heart that cries for your Truth to be heard. Trust the pain in your body where you might be hiding your Truth. Trust your intuition when something doesn't feel right. Trust the signs when they are there screaming at you. If something feels out of alignment, like it does not resonate, then it doesn't. If something interrupts your sleep to get your attention, then pay attention. These are all signs and symbols from your Higher Self and the Universe showing you and guiding you to a new place with a new perspective.

Trust your heart and let your heart fly free. Don't let the monkey in the mind take you away from your heart and all of its keepings. Trust the Divine heart inside you that knows the purest Truth of all. That you are Love and that you came from Love. Allow the tides within your heart to settle and find the shore of your sweetest Ease and Grace. Then allow the Ease and Grace that you naturally possess to flow abundantly. Allow your heart to be free to speak what it wants. Allow your hands to caress the Loved ones that you Love. Allow your stupendous heart to lead you always in all ways. Allow the desire for your heart's Truth inside you to ig-nite your passion. Your passion to lead, your passion to make way for all souls to evolve and your passion to spread the fire of Truth.

Allowing things to transpose other things can be very challenging work. To allow, to sit back and see and watch what will unfold in front of you can also be challenging. For if we truly let go, sit back and relax and watch, then sometimes what we see is not and will not be so pretty to look at. Some must go and pass through some very deep hardships to stir their Spirit and awaken their Soul. For the Light in them is screaming inside to be heard and it keeps getting drowned out and down with addictions and distractions and ego. This is not the path or the means to enter the realm of higher levels of awareness. There is enough of a strong conscious pull with all of the self-help gurus out there today, opening doors for people, for there to really be no excuse anymore to play small, to hide the pain nor to hurt others. We are in a time now where the consciousness is expanding rapidly and diligently within itself, and we are all getting swept along for the ride. It is truly a deeper time of awakening. To open our hearts and to pull back the moldy and moth-eaten layers that have been covering up our hearts. It is time to feel the deep yearning within your heart without any shame. It is time to feel all of the human heart and to stop the Spiritual bypassing and stories of the soul's learning and journey. It is time to shout from the rooftops and let the voice inside your heart be heard. It is time to let the deepest personal prayer in your heart be heard. It is time for the mask to come off and to let complete vulnerability be seen. It is time to let your heart guide you through and through. It is time to let your wildest dreams come out and be heard. It is time to become more clear and honest with your Self and what you want. What you need to make your Soul sing day to day. What you need to flourish in this life. What you need to feel honored, worshipped and nourished as a basic human need within Divine partnership.

What you allow your Self to feel in your heart. What you allow your Self to share from you heart with your Self. What you allow others to peek at if you feel like sharing your Divine Truth. For all that you truly know and feel is *your* Truth. And *your* Truth is what matters, as do the others. You may agree to disagree, but the Truth lies in allowing everyone's and all's personal experience. We are not to shut out and to close down anyone's feelings, for they are all important. Humanity lives, talks and listens on different wavelengths. We understand and interpret different experiences in different ways. Our nervous system translates them differently. Our memory distills things down to a "convenient Truth" at times. This is done as a way to protect the ego from melting at the hand of the Divine. For some, this Light, this Love is too much to bear. Those people take greater comfort in seeing and participating in the demise of others versus letting the Love and the Light melt them. That would be too threatening for the ego. There would be too much softness for their harshness. They would not know how to meet it and hold it. So instead of looking foolish and clumsy and asking for guidance, they stand their ground in the false security that they have forged around themselves and they begin to annihilate the same softness that has come to heal them.

They persecute the very thing that wants to help them and heal them. And in essence they end up annihilating themselves, for it is the Light of all that they end up persecuting, mistakenly forgetting that they are trying to destroy the same Light that lives and dwells within themselves. This is where self-sabotage comes in. It appears to be used and worn as a protective sword, but alas, it is anything but.

Download Twenty-Eight

So the freedom that you might find your Self-seeking is a freedom that already lives and breathes within you. It lives and breathes in your heart. It also lives and breathes in your Soul. It is a calling and a yearning deep inside you that wants to be let out. It wants to scream and shout from the rooftops and it wants to sing its highest and truest note and song. It wants to feather its own nest with the words from its heart and Soul. It wants to sing the loudest note to its own heart that can only be heard by the very same heart it sings to. For it does not matter the Truth that one is telling or singing for the most important thing is that it is that heart's Truth.

So, how can we lean back and honor all? How we can create more space in our minds and in our hearts for all that is out there? For there is really only one Truth and that is the Light of the Truth of God and in that, everything lives. That is what Truth is. So how can we, in what seems to look like a mixed-up world, make sense of *it* all. We can't really. You can try but you will most likely fail, just as those great philosophers who came before you. They tried to crack the code. They tried to crack the matrix. They came up with the most incredible and amazing formulas. They came up with the most fascinating and mind-expanding ideas and explanations for the psyche and human behavior. And they got very close, but no one *truly* cracked the code. Because it is not *meant* to be cracked. The code to the matrix is not as simple as picking a blue pill or a red pill as Hollywood might like you fantasize about. The mind will spend large amounts of time and energy discussing, theorizing, understanding and confusing schemes to help understand and explain behaviors of the mind. It ends up with a huge spectrum of disordered labels and yet is never able to find a remedy or a cure. It's like an animal chasing its tail. It is fun for a time but after a while, you get a little dizzy and eventually you feel exhausted.

So then it becomes time. The time then beckons to come back to the heart. To come back to the place in your body where your breath lives and your heart breathes its own life. Yes, your heart breathes its own rhythm. Your heart breathes its own Light. As the word breath translated from Latin is Spiritus. This is where you can find your Light, in your breath. Allow your breath to breath you. Allow your breath to move you. Allow your breath to ground you. Allow your breath to guide you. Allow your breath to heal you. Allow your breath to show you and to teach you. Allow the breath to be a flashlight in the dark corners of your heart where your pain sits, pain that you will heal.

Allow your breath to move you into higher states of awareness within your Self. And then you allow it to move you to higher states of awareness with others. It can and will move us into a less judgmental place. It can and will move us into a gentler place within our hearts. It can and will move us into a place where Love and Compassion sits and grows. Compassion is grown from seeds of understanding. It is very difficult to offer Compassion to another if we cannot offer Compassion to our selves.

Your scribe has a very compassionate heart for others as she dived deeply into the pain within her own heart and brought it out of the darkness. She has quelled her judgments for other's unsavory behaviors through the portal of understanding and therefore Compassion. Even when she has experienced flaming arrows thrown at her from someone so near and dear to her heart. From the ashes of torturous grief, insidious sexual abuse and mental abuse she has risen every time. And every time her wings have been burned, they eventually always heal. They behold scars to her beautiful and they allow her to soar higher and higher than ever before. They allow her as I have to give her the charge to walk with the knowledge and wisdom for healing and forgiveness. She *does* understand some of the code of this human matrix and I have therefore given her the duty and task of the education of those of higher spiritual learning to impart this wisdom. It is a new and balanced wisdom, if you will, that embodies the body, the heart, the mind and the Spirit. It is a new story about honoring all equally as they are all connected together and are all an integral part of you and all of humanity. It is the way through the proverbial door if you will. It is the way to honoring you and Life more purely. Part of this wisdom is acknowledging that all of these parts are the portals to an enriched and enchanted Life here on Earth. When these four elements are fully integrated, the Soul feels much more of its natural state, which is Love, Bliss, Happiness and Peace.

When these four elements are not in harmony, you will not be able to feel calm and really settle.

So, each day must be met with the knowledge that you are made up of these four parts and that it is your personal duty to meet these four elements within you with a deep honor, love, care and respect. For if you don't, then who will? Who will tend to your cut knee? Who will feed your hungry tummy? Who will hold your hand when you feel afraid? Who will hold you when you are down and there is no one around? Who will pray for you and your Spirit if you don't pray for your Self? Imagine if we could all take better care of ourselves, how we would place fewer expectations and demands on others in ways that pressure those we Love and care for the most?

This is the ultimate freedom. When you can know and feel that you are fully responsible for your own self-care and how that spans across all four elements. This is what it means to be free and to also place less demand on others around us. This too is freedom. Because in essence, this is a form of brutality, but not in the way it sounds. It is a brutality of sorts as it enables one and enforces one to be a bully, in a way. A bully comes from a place of needing something and wanting something. They have a pain inside them that is reflective of a need that is not being met or satisfied. Sometimes the need is great, like an emotional void, and sometimes it is food, shelter, water and sex. Now, when *all* of these things come together—and at times, they will—a brutality will show its head. And over the deep needs that have been ignored for so long, a deep scab has formed. These scabs will come and go representing the mental scars that the trauma has left. Because the trauma is the seeds of all "evil," if you will. The trauma can run so deep for so long without being tended that it actually begins to form a protective layer in the form of a personality. These personalities have been categorized by mental health experts, but the trauma runs deeper than that. The trauma runs a river deep into the Soul that can and will manifest at the Soul level. What this looks like is horrific. Those on the receiving end will experience a Machiavellian character that has been honed and shaped by severe and traumatic pain.

These traumas strike and run deep. These traumas do not hold anything back when they get triggered for healing. They will reek like death warmed over trying to draw you out of your hiding places while looking for vengeance. The revenge becomes a sport to feed the hungry negative ego, as the supply that you once provided is now gone. They are hungry. The trauma is hungry. It needs to eat. It needs to be fed. For without a supply or food source, it will fly around nitpicking and starting to tear apart others around them for no apparent reason. Because they are unable to feel and process their emotional pain and trauma they will regurgitate it onto others and onto nearly anyone who is standing, present and able to receive it. Meaning if they are breathing, they become the perfect target, so that means it could and will be anyone.

Download Twenty-Nine

But as of your now, things are passing around you and through you. As you gather up your personal sword to fight the injustice that lives and breathes inside you, you become your own hero to your own story.

You begin to see that shape and form of any harm that has come to you and any harm that you have placed upon others. You will temper these harms with the wit and will of your heart. You will see the tempest inside you rise with fury. A fury so great that they will besiege you to stand down and bow humbly to your authentic Self, to your Soul. Your Soul will beckon you from all of the corners of your somewhat circular mind. Your Soul will cry out to you and beg for your Mercy. It will beg for you to have Mercy on your own heart. It will beg you to rid your Self of your own judgments. And it will beg for you to shine your Light more brightly than you did yesterday.

So heed to the voice of your Soul. Honor your Soul. Cherish your Soul. Hold your Soul as though it were a baby chick, so tender, young, innocent and delicate. For the Soul is not eternal. It can be harmed and it *has* been harmed. That is why now is the time of Soul repair, if you will.

There are more healers and psychics on the planet than ever before. Yoga has taken over the West. All in the name of healing the Soul. The Soul's traumas, dramas, patterns and beliefs. This work is a similar approach to healing your current childhood wounds or the wounds of the heart. But now, we have arrived to a time where we have been preparing to heal the wound of the Soul and to also heal the wound of the collective Soul.

This is a trinity of sorts. The Heart, the Soul and the Collective Soul. The Collective Soul carries a collective wound, meaning a wound that all of humanity carries at some level. This can be explained as being a core belief of the Soul instead of the unconscious mind. You can and will find it, however, in the collective unconscious mind and the individual unconscious mind. There are many imprints that we carry at all three of these levels of programming and they are asking to be healed. To be integrated and vanquished. This is the new trinity of healing through the sacred feminine. The methodology for this will be shared in another form.

In the now, there is a call that comes from a place that requires and is asking for an even deeper understanding. The understanding that is being asked of us is to be more open to hearing the cry and the calls from our own hearts. To not be afraid of what we truly want. To not temper our heart's desires with limitations and bindings around its wings. Imagine it like a dove that just wants to fly free, that wants to live in Peace and wants to leave fear far behind in the winds of change as it soars high above its beloved playground where it spent time, practicing, learning, understanding, healing, contemplating. And as soon as it was nudged out of the nest to go off and live on its own, it knew, then and only then, how to fly free, because it had time to practice and because it was time.

Just as our Souls have had time to practice this path or way we call Life over and over, again and again. We have come to a resting place where our Souls are exhausted from the repeating lessons on the Karmic wheel of suffering. We are in a time where a door is opening for us to enter through and end this heavy time of Karmic suffering. To move into a place and time of ending each and every Soul's suffering.

There is a Spiritual teaching floating about that "you chose this experience" for your soul's growth. Did you?

Do you remember choosing? How do you really know that? Did you choose to contemplate and adopt the idea because it sounded good and there was no other alternative at that time to believe? The other newer teaching is that "You were chosen for this." They might both be true, and there is another idea to offer.

What if you were "sent" here to return all of the karmic grey matter to its rightful owner? What if everything you have been processing and healing is not truly yours?

How do you really know it is yours anyway? For example, where did the original idea come from that you feel you are not worthy of the most pure Divine, unconditionally loving Love? Perhaps this is truly the original sin. That we fell from Love. Perhaps we fell from Heaven so that we could transcend all of the grey-area thinking on a planet called Earth. Perhaps we were called here to this planet to help heal the "living hell" of the Karmic wheel of suffering?

What if you, what if *we* are not here to heal anything that isn't ours? What if we can just go straight to root, or straight to the original rotten seed, of the original sin? What if it wasn't a human who committed the original sin but an Angel? A Dark Angel?

What if an Angel became a Dark Angel as he chose to walk away from the right hand of the All-Loving God as he fell from Heaven to Earth? What if he cursed the planet with Karma so that anyone who comes here shall suffer like he felt he was suffering by falling from Heaven? What if that curse is the *only* reason any being here on Earth is wrought with Karmic Suffering? What if all of the other allegories are an illusion? What if suffering is an illusion and we are all crucifying ourselves? How, do you ask? Because we are processing suffering that is not ours to process. It is all an illusion because it is nothing more than a curse.

How would that change things? Would we make different choices? Would we be more responsive to Life and circumstance around us? Would you look at humanity as a whole so differently? Would we try to figure out a way to undo the curse? Is that even possible? It *is* possible and this is the time that there has been such a rapid accumulation of Light being anchored on the planet, that the new age has finally come upon us to heal this curse for good, for keeps.

This knot might seem too hard to untie, but it *is* possible. It is possible with a ton of will and determination on the planet. It needs to and will become a movement. It is called a movement because it is just that. People, humanity will feel and be moved by their hearts and Souls to finally put a stop to this Karmic atrocity so that *all* beings on this planet we call Earth can be free of their Karmic suffering.

I repeat…*all* beings will be relieved of their Karmic suffering, for it is a lie. It is not the way God wanted things to be here on this planet. It was a wrench in the plans, if you will. One might be pondering how did this happen under God's will or his watch. You see, God, knew this was going to happen, for God sees and knows everything. So even this wrench was a part of the plan, *and* it has now gone too far. It is time for things to come back into balance and to *re*-establish Heaven on Earth. For Earth was meant to be a colony of Heaven, if you will.

Download Thirty

And now the new times have arrived and settled and are settling in the hearts of so many. We have and we will have a new passage to follow and that passage is a new passage into the heart. It is a direct passage into the heart of the unknown. It is a direct passage into the river of the Divine Heart. And the river of the Divine Heart is not outside of us, it is in us. You are worthy of it and it is worthy of you. For you are One and the same. Don't you see, my cherished and Loved One, you are the Divine walking, you are the Divine speaking, you are the Divine feeling. All that you feel is the custard and the mustard. All that you feel is equal in its Divinity. For everything is a part of the Divine. Once you awaken to this, you become less judgmental of your Self and others, and you realize and see that there truly is a collective mind that speaks for everyone and everyone speaks for it.

The remedy to correct the bitter thoughts and words is to receive and ignite your gift of free choice and free will. Once you do the very deep work of awakening and feeling all the less savory and lower vibrational feelings you feel inside you, then and only then can you be free of this proverbial hell. For there is no shortcut. You *must* get up close and personal with your feelings of all without any judgment. You cannot go around your feelings.

You should not ask others to feel them for you as you will not be allowed into Heaven if you do not feel all of your feels. The Heaven that I am referring to is the Heaven on Earth. This is the second coming and the second creation. Where you move with Peace in your heart, mind, body and Spirit every step you take. Where people around you will see and feel your peacefulness. Where those others will ask you how you are while truly desiring to know how to obtain what you are emanating. They want to know how to alleviate their suffering like you have. They want to know how to stop the abuse like you have. They want to know Kindness and Compassion like you do. They want to be able to serve like you do. They want to move like you do. They want to move with Ease and Grace into a new way of being. They want their hearts to dance the dance that has been waiting for them. But so many don't know how, so we must teach them and we must show them, dear One.

The time has come for you to gather your things and to create a new movement. To create a new movement deep into the heart of the Divine, not with a false entry card but because you have survived thrashings of the Spirit and you have worked so diligently to cut the cords of deceit, punishment and curses time and time again. You have pushed beyond all measure those who have tried to drown you over and over, literally and metaphorically. You have come to a new time, a new place where it is now your turn to shine, to be seen and to be heard. This movement will be shared again and again and with more energetic transfusions and writings. These writings are so infused with sharing the frequency that is being knitted between the lines. Think of it as a code from the new Divine matrix. Think of it as a new software program that has now arrived to upgrade your programming. Think of it as a new way of thinking and being. Think of it and know it as an antidote. Think of it as a very necessary step in the evolution of the human heart and Spirit as we return the heartland of the Spirit, and as we return home. You will find that there will be guided audio-only meditations available through the app Insight Timer. It is free and easy to navigate. Simply search for Jesus Unplugged.

We want to extend to you and for you to feel full in your heart of the deep and sincere Gratitude we have for you and your reading, for taking the time thus far. Your heart, your Love, your presence and your Soul are now infused in a whole new way. You now have a new code. Enjoy it and go out and share it! Remember to anchor it with the meditations when you feel called in your heart or when you are perhaps unable to feel your own heart.

We thank your/our scribe, for we have tested here beyond testing and she has passed many a test with flying colors. Her heart is still healing while all of this has been stirring. It has helped and it has challenged her and for that we want you to understand and acknowledge her Strength, her Wisdom, her Valour and her Grace. She could have left. Most would have left, but she stayed. Rising again and again like a phoenix from the ashes, always seeking, always pushing the sound barrier of the human heart. And she now gets to rest. She now gets to play and finally feel safe, for she has earned it.

We embrace her, we bow to her and we above all admire her beauty and her poise. She has managed. We don't know humanly how, but she has. We have learned from her that beings can be more Enlightened in a body than without, and that societal rules can and will be broken when needed. We have learned how to nurture the human Spirit, for it requires a different care while in the body. And we have learned how true strength lives in the Spirit and the heart and cannot be measured by the muscles one wears.

Her tenacity is contagious. That is the point. She has crafted an authentic map because she *has* spent time and due diligence walking the uncharted terrain and territory. Please use this map and guide as a Spiritual and heart-based healing modality on your deeper path of awakening to your most authentic and sensitive Self.

Follow our/your scribe on a Podcast designed for live one-on-one coaching. There is an even more potent frequency transmitted through her voice and direct connection. You may receive her as well for hands-on healing when she is available. A short amount of time will do. She will lay your hands on your feet, your heart and your head. That will suffice. No words will be spoken so as not to engage the mind while the healing is being transmitted. No photos will be allowed or taken, please. We must respect the mission and keep the purity of the space intact.

Where there is a will, there is a way. This way is the new way. Trust the process and the way. Trust the callings when you hear and feel them.

We bid you farewell for now from this written page. There will be more soon.

Know that the "we" we speak of are a group of beings of Love and Compassion. Some of you know them as Angels and Cupids. Do not fear, for they are helpers.

Thank you. We love you. You are always held near in our hearts.

J.

Acknowledgements

I feel so much gratitude and awe for those people and forces that have all been a part of birthing this book. It certainly has taken a village. I cannot possibly mention all but suffice it to say that whether you are a new friend or an old friend, a foe or a part of my family, there are threads of all of you in this book. My experiences with all of your unique souls have made this personal journey possible. The finer touches must be credited to my Higher Power, to God (with a big G) and to Jesus. For without them I am sure I would probably not be here. I am humbled and I bow in gratitude to the generosity of Life and I have learned to respect the thorns in order to receive the rose.

To my darling oldest daughter, whom without her strength and her Love these pages would be blank. She has been one of my greatest teachers and steady companions as we grow and play together. To my youngest daughter, she has brought me the strongest medicine I have ever had to swallow. I am grateful for those lessons too.

As this book was being completed, I was really broken open with back surgery, broken promises and a broken engagement all within the last year. Those scars are too in these pages and I feel that it is these scars that we all bear to our beautiful.

To Anna David at Launch Pad Publishing and Ryan Aliapoulios, my co-writer, who managed to perfectly weave together the parts of my story that made the most sense to share with you, the reader, I thank you both.

My hope and intent is that this book and my story will open a different door to healing for your body, mind, heart and Spirit.

At the end of the day, there is no set path—but there is a path. Follow your heart and you will always find your higher Truth. Ask your Truth to meet where you are now. Join hand in hand and walk together, forward, bravely and all will be well.

Know that you are never truly alone and that you are always Loved.

In gratitude for you reading these pages, my wish is that you get ten-fold back from these words, sentiments and sharings.

Infinite warm blessings to you and your Loved Ones,

Rachel

Manufactured by Amazon.ca
Bolton, ON

11772447R00136